THE
PROPHECIES

A JOURNEY TO THE END OF TIME . . .

The Lord's Offer

Come unto Me,
all you who labor and are heavy laden,
and I will give you rest.

Take My yoke upon you
and learn of Me . . .
for I am meek and lowly in heart,
and you shall find rest unto your souls.

For My yoke is easy
and My burden is light.

Matt 11:28-30

The Prophecies: A Journey to the End of Time
Copyright © by Craig Crawford
All rights reserved.

ISBN 10 1500650196
ISBN 13 9781500650193

Library of Congress Catalog Card Number: 99-65124

Thanks to Minor White for "Structural Engineering" assistance

Printed in the United States of America

First Published 1999
Revised Edition 2014

Published by Prophecy Press

99 1

The following trademarks appear in this book: CNN, MTV, ABC, CBS, NBC, HBO, PBS, Time Warner, Disney, Buena Vista Pictures.

This book contains only a select sampling of the many, many hundreds of prophecies found in the Bible . . .

CONTENTS

From the Beginning . . .

*"In the beginning
God created the heavens and the Earth."*

Genesis 1:1

To the End . . .

*"Now I saw a new heaven and a new Earth,
for the first heaven and the first earth
had passed away."*

Revelation 21:1

OVERVIEW

*O*ur prophetic voyage through time will carry us from the mystery of the Messiah and the remarkable prophecies He fulfilled, to the terrors of the Apocalypse . . . and beyond. We will journey into the future and look at our destiny through the eyes of the prophets. The voyage is extraordinary.

Our *earthly* destiny could well be determined by whether we *are* in "that generation" which will draw the world down into the terrifying darkness of the coming Apocalypse . . .

Our *eternal* destiny is solely dependent on whether the awesome message the Bible reveals concerning our future *after* this short life on Earth is true. It is either true or false. We will find the implications of God's message are not trivial . . . *they are staggering!*

The Bible says only God knows "the end from the beginning." God uses prophecy to prove He *is* who He says He is, and to authenticate His message. The Bible is unlike any other book ever written. There is no other book like it. Prophecies found in the Bible are there for a reason. Prophecies allow the diligent and the skeptical to test God's word. Warnings are given so we will draw close to Him *before* the coming time of trouble. He will shelter and protect all who draw near.

This book is written on the firm belief that God says what He means and means what He says . . .

> "Search from the book of the LORD, and read:
> *Not one of these [prophecies] shall fail*;
> *Not one* shall lack her mate."   (Isaiah 34:16)

Now, let's begin our journey through time . . . *God's time.*

1

"For I am God, and there is no other.

I am God, and there is none like me,

Declaring the end from the beginning,

and from ancient times

things that are not yet done . . ."

Isaiah 46:9-10

MESSIAH

THE MYSTERY OF GOD

*"Then He (Jesus) said to them,
'These are the words which I spoke to you
while I was still with you, that all things
must be fulfilled which were written
in the Law of Moses and the Prophets
and the Psalms concerning Me.'
And He opened their understanding,
that they might comprehend the
Scriptures."*

Luke 24:44-45

MESSIAH: THE MYSTERY OF GOD

Christ is His Title. Messiah in the Hebrew . . . Christ in the Greek. He is the Alpha and the Omega. He is the beginning. He is the end. The Kingdom of Heaven has a King. He *is* the King. He stepped forth from Eternity to dwell with man, as a man. Every book in the Bible mysteriously points toward Him. Israel was removed from the Land when they rejected Him. Israel has been brought back into the Land to witness His return. His past is our past and *His future is our future* . . .

The Bible is God's personal message to Man. Although written over a vast number of years, it is perfectly integrated and consistent, showing the design of a *single* Author directing chosen men to write down His words. To prove that God *is* who He says He is, and to set the Bible apart from all other "religions" which would rise, God had His prophets write down, in detail, events that were going to happen in the future. Jesus said, *"Search the scriptures, for they testify of Me."* God tells us He will do nothing significant affecting the nation Israel or the world without first providing a warning, or warnings in advance, through His prophets . . .

> "Surely the Lord GOD does nothing,
> unless He reveals His secret to His servants the prophets."
> (Amos 3:7)

If this is true (and the Bible tells us that God cannot lie) then God would have prepared Israel for the Messiah *and* He would have included enough detail to insure that there could be no question as to His identity. The Apostles tell us that even though the accounts documented by them were seen by many thousands of eyewitnesses, *"We have even the more sure word of prophecy,"* Jesus was in fact the Christ, the promised Messiah. What did they mean by that . . .

7

The ancient Holy scriptures, sometimes called the "Old Testament," from which the following prophecies are taken, were written between 400 to 2,000 years *before* Christ (B.C.) and were later translated from the Hebrew into Greek by 72 Jewish priests and scholars who were brought together sometime around *270 B.C.* *So, these prophecies were in writing and being translated from Hebrew into Greek almost three hundred years before Christ was even born!*

This Hebrew to Greek translation of the ancient Holy Scriptures is called the "Septuagint," and is well documented in both Jewish and secular history.

What prophetic details did God weave into the ancient Holy Scriptures concerning the coming Messiah?

- *He would be born of a virgin*

   "Behold, the virgin shall conceive and bear a Son,
   and shall call His name Immanuel" (Isaiah 7:14)
   [Immanuel means *"God is with us"*]

- *He would be the Son of God*

   "For unto us a Child is born, unto us a Son is given,
   and His name will be called . . . Mighty God,
   Everlasting Father, Prince of Peace." (Isaiah 9:6)

- *He would be born in Bethlehem . . .*
   after leaving His place in Eternity

   "But you, O Bethlehem Ephrathah,
   though you are little among the thousands of Judah,
   Yet out of you shall come forth to Me The One to be
   ruler in Israel, Whose goings forth have been
   from of old, *from everlasting."* (Micah 5:2)

- *He would ride triumphantly into Jerusalem . . .*
  yet meek and lowly . . . riding on a donkey

  "Rejoice greatly, O daughter of Zion [Israel]!
  Behold, your King is coming to you;
  He is just and having salvation,
  yet He is lowly and riding on a donkey."
      (Zechariah 9:9)

- *He would be betrayed by a friend*

  "Even my own familiar friend in whom I trusted, who
  ate my bread, has lifted up his heel against me."
      (Psalm 41:9)

- *They would set a price on Him of 30 pieces of silver . . .*
  which would then be thrown into the potter's field

  "So they weighed out for my wages thirty pieces of silver.
  And the LORD said to me, 'Throw it to the potter' -
  that princely price they set on me."   (Zechariah 11:12-13)

- *He would be meek and humble*

  "He had no beauty or majesty to attract us to him,
  nothing in his appearance that we should desire him."
      (Isaiah 53:2 NIV)

- *We would despise Him and reject Him . . .*
  He would feel the pain of rejection

  "He is despised and rejected by men,
  A Man of sorrows and acquainted with grief."
      (Isaiah 53:3)

9

- *We would turn our backs on Him and look the other way as he went by*

    "And we hid, as it were, our faces from Him;
      He was despised, and we did not esteem Him." (Isaiah 53:3)

- *He would be rejected by Israel*

    "The Redeemer of Israel, their Holy One,
      To Him whom man despises,
      To Him whom the nation abhors." (Isaiah 49:7)

- *He would suffer . . . brutally beaten and bloodied*

    "So His appearance was marred more than any man"
        (Isaiah 52:14)

- *He would be beaten, bloodied and would die for **our** sins*

    "But He was wounded for our transgressions,
    He was bruised for our iniquities;
    The chastisement for our peace was upon Him,
    And by His stripes [whip lashes] we are healed.
    And the LORD has laid on Him the iniquity [sin] of us all."
        (Isaiah 53:5-7)

- *Yet, He would remain silent during His ordeal*

    "He was led as a lamb to the slaughter,
    And as a sheep before its shearers is silent,
    So He opened not His mouth." (Isaiah 53:7)

- *He would be Crucified . . . a torturous and agonizing death*

  "All My bones are out of joint . . .
  My tongue clings to My jaws;
  They pierced My hands and My feet,
  They look and stare at Me."   (Psalm 22:14, 15, 16, 17)

- *He would have stakes . . . nails . . . driven through his hands*

  "And someone will say to Him,
  'What are these wounds in your hands?'
  Then He will answer,
  'Those with which I was wounded
  in the house of my friends.'"   (Zech 13:6)

- *He would be mocked during His time of suffering and death*

  "A reproach of men and despised of the people,
  They shoot out the lip, they shake the head, saying
  'He trusted in the Lord, let Him rescue Him;'"
  (Psalm 22:7-8)

- *They would cast lots for His clothes*

  "They divide my garments among them,
    and for My garments they cast lots."   (Psalm 22:18)

- *He who knew no sin would be made sin for us . . .*

  "My God, My God, why have You forsaken me?"
      (Psalm 22:1 . . . Matt 27:46)

With these words from the Cross, Jesus was pointing the Jewish
leaders to Psalm 22 . . .

The Jewish leaders who were gathered around the Cross knew the Scriptures well. Psalm 22 is a detailed prophecy foretelling the death of Jesus, the Messiah, on the Cross, written *a thousand* years before the Cross and written *centuries before* this form of execution was even invented - written when the Jewish form of execution was *stoning*.

- *His side would be pierced*

    "Then they will look upon Me whom they have pierced;
    they will mourn for Him as one mourns for his only son,
    and grieve for Him as one grieves for a firstborn."
        (Zech 12:10 . . . a prophecy of His Return)

- *He would be buried in a rich man's grave*

    "He was buried like a criminal in a rich man's grave;"
        (Isaiah 53:9)

- *He was innocent . . . without guilt . . . without sin*

    "But he had done no wrong,
    and he had never spoken an evil word."
        (Isaiah 53:9)

- *He would be raised from the dead*

    "For You will not leave my soul in Sheol [Hell],
    Nor will You allow Your Holy One
    to see corruption [decompose]."
        (Ps 16:10)

- *He would be a savior to all peoples, including Jews and non-Jews alike, thus fulfilling the Abrahamic Covenant*

  "I will also give You as a light to the Gentiles,
  That You should be My salvation
  to the ends of the Earth."
  (Isaiah 49:6)

- *He would be The Sacrifice for all of our sins*

  "And He bore the sin of many . . ."
  (Isaiah 53:12)

- *The Cross was part of God's Plan . . . so that we might live and be spared from the second death, which the Bible says is the utter darkness and torment of Hell . . .*

  "Yet it was the Lord's good plan to bruise him;
  put Him to grief, make His soul an offering for sin . . ."
  (Isaiah 53:10, KJV paraphrased)

- *He would then return to His place in Heaven, until . . .*

  "I [the LORD] will return again to My place
  until they [Israel] acknowledge their offense.
  Then they will seek My face;
  in their affliction [the Tribulation]
  they will diligently seek Me" . . .
  (Hosea 5:15)

For the LORD to *return* to His place means that He had to have *left* His place. One requirement that must be met before He can return to Earth is for the people of Israel to "acknowledge their offense." (Notice that the word <u>offense</u> is singular, not plural, and it is specific.) This means that Israel must acknowledge their rejection of the Messiah and pray, as a nation, for His return. We are told this will be fulfilled at the very end of the Tribulation. God will fulfill all of His covenants with the nation Israel.

• *When the Word and the prophecies became flesh . . .*

"Now when they had fulfilled
all that was written concerning Him,
they took Him down from the tree
and laid Him in a tomb.
But God raised Him from the dead.
He was seen for many days by those
who came up with Him from Galilee to Jerusalem,
who are His witnesses to the people." (Acts 13:29-31)

Then He [Jesus] said to them,
"These are the words which I spoke to you while I was
still with you, that all things must be fulfilled
which were written in the Law of Moses
and the Prophets and the Psalms concerning Me."
And He opened their understanding,
that they might comprehend the Scriptures.
Then He said to them, *"Thus it is written,
and thus it was necessary* for the Christ [Messiah]
to suffer and to rise from the dead the third day,
and that repentance and remission of sins
should be preached in His name to all nations,
beginning at Jerusalem."
    (Luke 24:44-47)

The first prophecy found in the Bible is spoken by God to Adam, Eve, and Satan, in the Garden of Eden . . .

> "I will put enmity [hatred]
> between you [Satan] and the woman [Eve],
> And between your seed [the Antichrist] and her Seed [the Christ];
> He shall bruise your head, and you shall bruise His heel."
> (Gen 3:15)

This first prophecy is a prophecy of the Messiah. It also sets the stage for Satan's hatred against mankind. In the book of Job, we find Satan attacks us *and* our families, bringing sickness, death, and distress into our lives to try to separate us from God . . . to "curse God and die." Also, there are other prophecies found in the Bible concerning this prophetic "head" wound the coming "Antichrist" will sustain and appear to be "resurrected" from.

In this prophecy we are told the seed of the woman, the Messiah (the Christ), would have his heel bruised. If you study the physical trauma associated with Crucifixion, you soon find it was designed to cause extreme pain and torment before death. The word "excruciating" comes from the root word "crucify." Crucifixion was a cruel, slow, agonizing, and tortuous form of execution designed to kill through slow suffocation. The shoulders of the person being crucified would dislocate and separate. The only way the person nailed to the Cross could breathe (or speak) would be to gather as much strength as they could and try to stand up on the nail or the spike that had been driven through their feet. The feet were severely bent forward and pressed together in order to nail them to the Cross. When the feet were nailed securely to the Cross, one heel would be pressed tightly against the wood of the Cross. So, in order to breathe or to speak, the person nailed to the Cross had to put all of their weight on the heel and the large spike that had been driven through the feet in order to stand up far enough to gasp for breath. This incredibly tortuous process would painfully bruise that heel. Also, we are told that Jesus was scourged by the Romans before He was crucified. These "stripes" He took on His back were another form of cruel punishment derived by the powers of the day. The Roman "whip" used for scourging was small with pieces of metal and bone attached. The prisoner's back was stretched tight as He, in this case, Jesus, was tied to a post. The Roman whip was designed to dig into the skin of the back and then tear the skin away from the bone. By the time Jesus was crucified the skin of His back that had been torn from the "stripes" would have been hanging loosely off of the bone like a tattered cloth. Take a moment to consider the amount of pain shooting through the body of Christ as He struggled with dry, parched lips and gasping for breath to stand up by pressing down on that heel which was *nailed* to the Cross, causing His tattered back with its exposed bone to rub against the roughly hewn wood of His Cross in order to clearly speak those words . . . *"Father forgive them, for they know not what they do."*

Note to Christians: It is wrong and a blasphemy against God and Jesus to ever blame the Jews for Jesus' death. As one pastor put it, "If you are going to blame anybody blame *me*, for it was because of *my sins* that the Messiah stepped forth from Eternity and took on the form of Man, as the Son of Man . . . the Son of God, to suffer and die.

Believing Christians are taught to help Israel and her people . . .

> "Cursed be everyone who curses you [Israel],
> and blessed be those who bless you!" (Gen 27:29)

God has a *covenant* with Israel that will never be broken. He has revealed a *destiny* for Israel which will soon be completed.

God has declared a *new* covenant and destiny for a people to be drawn from the *whole* world, through His Messiah, *including* the children of Israel who recognize their Messiah *from Scripture*. This new covenant is a promise for all who believe in Him, and accept Him.

16

Another ancient prophecy "foreshadowing" the Cross . . .

We find another prophetic "foreshadowing" of the Cross in the book of Numbers, one of the five books of Moses . . .

> "So the LORD sent fiery serpents among the people,
> and they bit the people; and many of the people of Israel died.
> Therefore the people came to Moses, and said, 'We have sinned,
> for we have spoken against the LORD and against you;
> pray to the LORD that He take away the serpents from us.'
> So Moses prayed for the people.
> Then the LORD said to Moses,
> 'Make a fiery serpent, and set it on a pole;
> and it shall be that everyone who is bitten,
> when he looks at it, shall live.'
> So Moses made a bronze serpent, and put it on a pole;
> and so it was, if a serpent had bitten anyone,
> when he looked at the bronze serpent, he lived."
> (Num 21:6-9)

In the Bible, the serpent is used as a symbol for "sin," and bronze a symbol of "judgement," because bronze could withstand the fire. We find in this verse that once the people acknowledged their sin, they only needed to look upon the serpent on the pole to be healed and saved. We are told Jesus "became" sin, like that "fiery serpent" on the pole, for us . . .

> "For He made Him who knew no sin [Jesus on the Cross]
> *to be sin for us,* that we might become
> the righteousness of God in Him."
> (2 Cor 5:21)

Jesus points to this prophetic model of the serpent on the pole . . .

Jesus said, "And as Moses lifted up the serpent in the wilderness,
even so must the Son of Man be lifted up,
that whoever believes in Him should not perish
but have eternal life [in His Kingdom of Heaven].
For God so loved the world that He gave His only begotten Son,
that whoever believes in Him should not perish,
but have everlasting life [in Heaven].
For God did not send His Son into the world to condemn
the world, but that the world through Him might be saved."
[Saved from the *second* death . . . the agony and torment of hell]
(John 3:14-17)

It is interesting that after hearing the story of the serpent in the wilderness, the ancient Greeks adopted this sign of the serpent on the pole as their symbol for healing. The symbol is still used by our medical profession. You might note there is only *one* serpent on this ancient symbol, not two.

So, as those who looked upon the fiery serpent in the wilderness were saved from their sins, so will all who consider and believe in Jesus on the Cross be saved . . . and welcomed into His Kingdom of Heaven, forever.

The Promise of the Cross is available to everybody. The offer is extended to all. The early church included all - Jew, Roman, Ethiopian, Greek, rich and poor, men and women, centurion and rabbi, together, *as one.* They saw . . . they heard . . . *they believed.*

It was only after the Jews rejected their Messiah that the good news of this new covenant of God's grace would be offered to all people around the world. Christ died for *all* who believe, from Israel and the Nations.

18

A <u>remarkable</u> mathematical prophecy . . .

Daniel 9:24

"He [Messiah, the King] will be revealed
7 weeks + 62 weeks [these represent weeks of *years*]
after the commandment to rebuild Jerusalem *and its walls,*
then He [the Messiah] *will be cut-off.*"

- A mathematical prophecy . . .
  A week of years, *shabua* or *shabu'im* = 7 years

- "Cut-off". . . the actual Hebrew word used was *karath,*
  which literally means *"executed!"*

- The *"70th* Week" of this prophecy is yet future - See
  Armageddon.

This prophecy of the coming Messiah is both remarkable and
extremely precise. There were several orders to rebuild the *Temple,*
but, there was only *one* commandment to restore Jerusalem *and its
wall.* On March 14th, 445 BC, as confirmed by modern archaeology,
King Artexerxes I of Persia issued the commandment to rebuild
Jerusalem, *specifically including its wall* (see Nehemiah 1:2-9).

To translate the Babylonian/Persian 360 day years into days . . .

7 + 62 *weeks* of years = 69 years x *7* = 483 years
483 years x 360 days = 173,880 days in this prophecy

The prophet Daniel, *who lived 500 years before Jesus* (this prophecy
was later translated from Hebrew into Greek almost *300* years before
Jesus) wrote that from the day of the commandment to rebuild
Jerusalem *and its walls,* until the coming Prince *(the Messiah), would
be 173,880 days.*

Now, convert the 173,880 days found in this prophecy into 365.25 day solar years (the *.25* adjusts for *leap* years) . . .

$$173,880 \div 365.25 \text{ days } = \textbf{476 years}$$

To convert, divide by 365.25 (which adds the leap years), then add one year because there is no "0" B.C. or A.D. Then start counting on March 14, 445 B.C. and you *just happen* to arrive on *the very year, even the very day* of Jesus's triumphal entry into Jerusalem (Palm Sunday), as King, honored, yet lowly, *riding on a donkey* (See Zech 9:9) - *exactly* as the prophets said He would! On April 6th, 32 A.D. (10th day of Nisan on the Hebrew calendar) Jesus made His famous triumphal entry into Jerusalem, riding on a donkey. It was the *only day* that He *ever* allowed Himself to be honored as Messiah or King (Mark 11:1-12) as the people of Israel cried and sang "Hosanna to the Son of David [this is a Psalm of the Messiah], blessed is He who comes in the name of the LORD!" from Psalm 118.

A remarkable prophecy . . . simply count the years!

March 14, 445 B.C.	Order is issued to rebuild the wall
<u>*to* April 6, 32 A.D.</u>	Palm Sunday - Jesus welcomed, *as King!*
= 477 years	
<u>- 1 year</u>	*Subtract* one for no "0" A.D. or B.C.
= *476 years*	*Exactly!*

Or . . .

445 B.C.	Order is issued to rebuild the wall
+ 476 years	Number of years in Daniel's prophecy
<u>+ 1 year</u>	This way, we *add* one for no "0" year.
= *32 A.D.*	***The year Jesus was presented as Messiah, exactly when the Bible said He would!***

Who <u>else</u> in 32 - 33 A.D. fulfilled these many prophecies?

No one. Only Jesus of Nazareth . . . *the promised Messiah!*

Right after the "Triumphal Entry," Jesus wept over Jerusalem, knowing the people of Israel would ignore this prophecy and the other prophecies of the Messiah *which were so specific* that God would hold them accountable! *This is why the Temple was destroyed and the Jewish people were scattered and dispersed around the world* . . .

Jesus reveals a *new* prophecy and tells Israel *why* it would happen -

> "Now as He [Jesus] drew near,
> He saw the city [Jerusalem] and wept over it,
> saying, '*If you had known*, even you [the children of Israel],
> especially in this your day, [this day Daniel prophesied about]
> the things that make for your peace!
> But *now they are hidden* from your eyes.
> For days will come upon you when your enemies will build
> an embankment around you, surround you
> and close you in on every side, and level you,
> and your children within you, to the ground; and
> *they will not leave in you [the Temple] one stone upon another,*
> <u>because you did not know the time of your visitation.</u>'"
> (Luke 19:41-44)

Thus, within that generation, in 70 A.D., *38 years <u>after</u> Jesus was crucified*, Jerusalem *was* besieged and brutally destroyed when Titus Vespasian, with the Fifth, Tenth, Twelfth, and Fifteenth Roman Legions *did* build a Roman siege wall around the city, starving and slaughtering over a million Jews, and then *tore down the Temple, stone by stone,* to retrieve the gold that had melted when Roman soldiers (against orders) set the Temple on fire, thus leaving not one stone upon the other . . . *exactly as Jesus had prophesied.* The Romans then scattered and dispersed the Jews around the world.

21

The Scriptures tell us there are two roles the Messiah must fulfill:

First, as the *Passover Lamb of God . . .*
Whose blood on the Cross saves us from the "*second* death" (Hell)

Second, as *the Lion of Judah . . .*
To restore the Earth . . . the King of kings . . . *the Lord of lords.*

The Scriptures tell us the Messiah will return . . . twice:

First, "as a thief in the night" . . .
Mysteriously, to remove His Church [faithful believers] from Earth to shelter and protect them from the coming Apocalypse.

Second, "every eye shall see" . . .
When He returns to establish His just and fair rule over the world.

Remember . . .

We, as followers of Christ, are to be a separate people - a people of honor, strength, and courage. To obey Him, we must take the heart of a servant and be meek, humble, patient, kind, willing to forgive, willing to help and serve others, even our enemies. This requires much strength. This *is* strength. We must pray for His strength. Hold fast and endure in faith. God watches us, hears us, and knows our hearts. He is the God who lovingly offers a second (and third and fourth) chance. He waits patiently for us to return to Him, and will forgive us when we ask.

If there was any other way into Heaven . . .

Jesus knew what was about to happen when He prayed, *"If there is any other way"* three times in the garden the night before He was crucified. If there was, or is, any other way to gain entrance into Heaven other than believing in the One who paid our debt, then Jesus suffered and died *needlessly and in vain*, on the Cross. He lovingly laid down His life for you and for me.

> "The Lord is my shepherd . . ."
> (Psalm 23:1)

> And Jesus graciously tells us,
> "*I am* the good shepherd.
> The good shepherd gives his life for the sheep."
> (John 10:11)

It is interesting to note the only prophecies found in other religions are either based on prophecies *already* found in the Scriptures, or point to a powerful leader who someday will rise. God warns to beware of this false messiah who *will* soon rise and *will* deceive many. God also makes it very clear there would be only *one* real Messiah. If you are approached, or belong to a religion which denies Jesus is the Messiah, the Son of Man ... the Son of God, humbly ask them to show you the prophecies preparing the way and describing their prophet . . .

In the beginning was the Word . . .
and the Word was with God,
and the Word was God.

And the Word became flesh
and dwelt among us,
and we beheld His glory,
the glory as of the only begotten
of the Father . . .
full of grace and truth.

He was in the world,
the world was made through Him,
and the world did not know Him.

He came to His own,
and His own did not receive Him . . .

(Excerpted from the Book of John 1:1-14)

THE

RAPTURE

" Behold, I tell you a mystery:

We shall not all sleep,

but we shall all be changed -

in a moment,

in the twinkling of an eye . . . "

1 Cor 15:51-52

THE RAPTURE

*T*he Bible warns of a coming day when all who are found waiting in faith will be removed from Earth *in a moment*, in the "twinkling of an eye." What *is* this strange, bizarre, mysterious, prophecy all about?

The Scriptures tell us the Messiah will return . . . *twice:*

- *First, "as a thief in the night,"* to remove those who wait.
- *Second, "every eye shall see,"* in power and glory . . .

It might help to understand *why* Jesus feels it will be important to remove this group of believers from the Earth in such a decisive and startling way. We find the Rapture is somewhat analogous to a terrified mother yanking her young child off the railroad tracks just as the train goes thundering by. Prophet after prophet in the Bible warns us of a very specific period of time referred to by many names, including the "Great Tribulation" or the "Apocalypse" (which actually refers to the Revelation or "revealing"), when God is going to pour out His wrath on a violent, arrogant, and unbelieving world. We are told that those who believe in His Son and wait in faith are not appointed to this time of wrath . . .

> "And to wait for His Son from heaven,
> whom He raised from the dead, even *Jesus,*
> *who delivers us from the wrath to come."* (1 Thes 1:10)

> "*For God did not appoint us to wrath,*
> but to obtain salvation through our Lord Jesus Christ,
> who died for us, that whether we wake or sleep,
> we should live together with Him.
> Therefore comfort each other and edify one another,
> just as you also are doing." (1 Thes 5:9-11)

27

The actual word "rapture" is not found in most Bibles. The Greek word which was translated "caught up" in the English, was translated in the Latin as "*rapturo*." So, the term "rapture" comes from a *Latin* translation. In fact the Greek word actually used, which was translated in the King James version as "caught up" (1 Thes 4:17), is "*harpazo*" which easily could have been, or should have been translated, "to seize, to pluck away, or to take by force."

The "Rapture of the Church" *is* controversial. So, before we get started, please remember one important thing. Whether you believe the church will be "snatched away" *before* the great and awesome Day of the Lord, or in the *middle* of it, or at the *end* of it, or if you just don't know, doesn't really matter. *The only thing that matters is that you don't get left behind.* The door *will* be shut. This prophecy, or *any* prophecy, should not be a point of contention between believers. However, it is an interesting prophecy. The belief, or point of view expressed here, is that the Lord will remove His Church, which includes all who sincerely believe in Him, from the Earth *before* the great Tribulation. This view might be wrong. The view presented in this book also supports the belief that this generation *is* the generation of the Rapture and a worldwide body of faithful believers will be removed suddenly before the person or the identity of the Antichrist will be, or even *can be*, revealed. And since many feel this man who has been given many titles in the Bible, including the Antichrist, is probably alive today, it is worth the time to look at some of the verses found in the Bible which directly, or indirectly refer to this strange, forceful, prophetic event which we simply call *the Rapture* . . .

"Behold, I tell you a mystery:
We shall not all sleep,
but we shall all be changed--
in a moment, in the twinkling of an eye"

(1 Cor 15:51-52)

28

"For the Lord Himself will descend from heaven with a shout,
with the voice of an archangel, *and with the trumpet of God.*
And the dead in Christ will rise first.
Then we who are alive and remain
shall be caught up together with them in the clouds
to meet the Lord in the air.
And thus we shall always be with the Lord."   (1 Thes 4:16-18)

And Jesus said, "Let not your heart be troubled;
you believe in God, believe also in Me.
In My Father's house are many mansions [abiding places];
if it were not so, I would have told you.
I go to prepare a place for you.
And if I go and prepare a place for you,
I will come again and receive you to Myself;
that where I am, there you may be also."   (John 14:1 - 4)

"For in the time of trouble he shall hide me in His pavilion;
in the secret place of His tabernacle he shall hide me;
he shall set me high upon a rock."   (Ps 27:5)

"Come, *my people*, enter your chambers,
and shut your doors behind you;
hide yourself, as it were, for a little moment,
until the indignation [Tribulation] is past.
For behold, the LORD comes out of His place
to punish the inhabitants of the Earth for their iniquity;
the Earth will also disclose her blood,
and will no more cover her slain."   (Isa 26:20 - 21)

"Seek the LORD, all you meek of the Earth,
Who have upheld His justice.
Seek righteousness, seek humility.
*It may be that you will be hidden
in the day of the LORD'S anger."*
   (Zeph 2:3)

"Because you have kept My command to persevere,
*I also will keep you from the hour of trial
which shall come upon the whole world,*
to test those who dwell on the Earth."
"Behold, I come quickly!"
   (Rev 3:10-11)

"But of that day and hour no one knows,
no, not even the angels of heaven, but My Father only."
   (Matt 24:36)

"Then two men will be in the field:
one will be taken and the other left.
Two women will be grinding at the mill:
one will be taken and the other left."
"Watch therefore, for you do not know
what hour your Lord is coming."
   (Matt 24:40-42)

"Therefore you also be ready,
for the Son of Man is coming at an hour you do not expect."
   (Luke 12:40)

*"But concerning the times and the seasons, brethren,
you have no need that I should write to you.
For you yourselves know perfectly
that the day of the Lord so comes as a thief in the night."*
   (1 Thes 5:1-2)

Who will get "Raptured" and who will be left behind?

To simplify things, let's divide all of the people in the world into four groups:

1. Those who sincerely believe in Jesus Christ - Those who believe that "Christ died on the Cross for our sins, and that He was buried, and that He rose again the third day, according to the Scriptures" (1 Corinthians 15). All those who have accepted Him as their Lord and now wait in faith.

2. Those who call themselves Christians, but don't really believe these things and have no real faith in Jesus, God, or the Bible. Those who have never willingly opened the door of their heart to invite Jesus into their lives and accept Him as their Lord.

3. "The world." Those who do not believe and who ridicule, scoff at, or despise those who do. Those who deny Jesus as Lord and willfully reject His offer of forgiveness.

4. Israel. The children of Israel have a clear prophetic destiny. Watch Israel. Israel is God's timepiece and focus in prophecy.

It appears that only those believers in Group (1), the first group, will be "Raptured," and thus safely removed and hidden before the coming Apocalypse. Many pulpits and pews will still be filled. Many people will be left behind. The Bible warns of a coming world leader who will be revealed sometime after the Rapture. There are some who feel this coming world dictator may even try to convince those who are left on Earth that this missing segment of global population was kidnapped or removed by a much different kind of "force."

When will the Rapture take place?

We do not know, and we are told that *no* man will ever know the day or the hour. However, there doesn't appear to be anything left in prophecy that needs to be fulfilled before the Rapture can take place, so, it could easily happen any day . . .

The *Lord* says it could happen at any moment, "in the twinkling of an eye." He says it will happen at a time when the world will least expect it. We are told we should always be prepared by simply believing in Him and waiting for Him in faith. We are taught we should help prepare others.

After the Rapture . . . the door will then close.

A WARNING . . . THE PARABLE OF THE TEN VIRGINS

"Then the kingdom of heaven shall be likened to ten virgins,
who took their lamps and went out to meet the bridegroom.
Now five of them were wise, and five were foolish.
Those who were foolish took their lamps,
and took no oil with them,
but the wise took oil in their vessels with their lamps.

While the bridegroom was delayed, they all slumbered and slept.
And at midnight a cry was heard,
'Behold, the bridegroom is coming; go out to meet him!'
Then all those virgins arose and trimmed their lamps.
And the foolish said unto the wise,
'Give us some of your oil, for our lamps are gone out.'

But the wise answered, saying,
'No, lest there should not be enough for us and you;
but go rather to those who sell, and buy for yourselves.'
And while they went to buy, the bridegroom came,
and they that were ready went in with him to the wedding;
and the door was shut.

Afterward the other virgins came also saying, 'Lord, Lord, open to us.'
But he answered and said, 'Verily I say to you, I do not know you.'
"Watch therefore, for you know neither the day nor the hour
in which the Son of man is coming." (Matt 25:1-13)

Note: Throughout the Bible, certain symbols are used consistently as idioms or types. Consider the following . . .

- As a parable *and* a prophecy, the bridegroom represents Jesus.
- The 10 virgins represent those who call themselves Christians.
- The oil represents the Holy Spirit. God promises to fill all who sincerely believe and wait in faith with His Holy Spirit.

33

What does "Born again" mean?

Nicodemus, a powerful Jewish religious leader (who we find later *did* believe and accept Jesus as the promised Messiah) came to speak with Jesus one night . . .

"Jesus answered and said to him, 'Most assuredly, I say to you, *unless one is born again, he cannot see the kingdom of God.'*
Nicodemus said to Him, 'How can a man be born when he is old? Can he enter a second time into his mother's womb and be born?'
Jesus answered, 'Most assuredly, I say to you,
unless one is born of water *and* the Spirit,
he *cannot enter* the kingdom of God.
That which is born of the flesh is flesh,
and that which is born of the Spirit is spirit.'"
    (John 3:3-6)

We had no choice concerning our first birth, but to be born of the Spirit and into the Kingdom of Heaven *requires a conscious decision* on our part. The Bible says if we simply believe, sincerely and in faith, that Jesus died for our sins, was buried, then rose the third day, and sincerely accept Him as our Lord and invite Him into our lives, then we are "born again." Only *this* time, we are born of the *Spirit* and not of flesh. We are then told we will be filled with His Holy Spirit (the oil). This is God's Word and His Promise. Even while facing the difficult tests and trials we will find in our *earthly* lives, we can rest knowing our *eternal* destiny is assured.

The choice of our eternal destiny is made by us . . . not by God.

THE RISE

OF THE

ANTICHRIST

"The coming of the lawless one [Antichrist]

is according to the working of Satan,

with all power, signs,

and lying wonders"

II Th 2:7-9

THE RISE OF THE ANTICHRIST

God warns of a world leader who will soon rise and grow in power. He will begin by exerting control over a ten nation alliance in Europe. Three leaders or nations will then fall or will be subdued . . .

> "The ten horns are ten kings who shall arise from [out of]
> this kingdom [the Roman Empire - modern Europe].
> And another shall rise after them;
> he [the Antichrist] *shall be different* from the first ones,
> and shall subdue three kings . . ." (Dan 7:24) [The end begins]

This man will quickly consolidate power over Europe and then over the whole world through treaties and war. God warns this man will be empowered by Satan. He will lead the world into the Apocalypse. This coming world leader has been given many names and titles in the Bible, including one of the best known, yet most misleading - the Antichrist. Although he will be against *faithful* Christians and will mock God's law, the world will view him as a great leader and a man of peace. This man will be Satan's *counterfeit* messiah. He will use deception and lies to "spin" his web of deceit and to conceal his true motives. Prophecies hint this man will not be fully revealed until after the Rapture, when the "Restrainer" is taken out of the way . . .

> "For the mystery of lawlessness is already at work;
> *only He who now restrains* [the Holy Spirit]
> will do so *until* He is taken out of the way.
>
> *And then* the lawless one [Antichrist] will be revealed,
> whom the Lord will consume with the breath of His mouth
> and destroy with the brightness of His coming.
>
> The coming of the lawless one [Antichrist]
> is according to the working of Satan,
> with all power, signs [miracles], and lying wonders" (II Th 2:7-9)

"He who now restrains" . . .

We are told that all who believe Christ died for their sins, was buried, then raised from the dead, and accept Him as Lord are "born again," and are then indwelt by the Holy Spirit. According to the Bible, you cannot separate the Holy Spirit from the believing Christian. This is God's promise. So, in order to remove "He who now restrains" (the Holy Spirit), God must also remove the body of believers who are alive at that time. This is why many believe the man some call the Antichrist *cannot* be revealed until *after* the Rapture of the Church. Since we are told that this coming world leader will be indwelt by the power and spirit of Satan, we should learn a little bit about Satan.

Satan . . .

The Bible has a lot to say about this creature, Satan. God wants us to have knowledge of the enemy. God wants us to know Satan is real and he is powerful. We are told he was the "anointed Cherub who covers." The diligent student of the Bible will discover that Cherubim (plural form of cherub) are at the highest level of rank and order of those created beings called angels. Cherubim are not pudgy little babies with wings as shown in some art. They are powerful! We only know of five that were created. Four now surround the throne of God and the fifth was once the head of this rank until he became filled with violence and pride. We find in the Bible God goes out of His way to make sure we know Satan was created. We also find in the Bible that God, through the Holy Spirit, goes out of His way to make sure we know Jesus Christ was *not* created. As we are told in the book of John, "Jesus was the Word that became flesh, and the Word was with God and the Word *was* God and by Him *all* things were created." God stepped out of Eternity and placed His Spirit into the form of man, as the Son of Man . . . as the Son of God. Satan, with his many names and titles, is the most powerful creature ever created. Jesus defeated Satan at the Cross. The only "person" powerful enough to defeat Satan had to be God Himself, who created Satan. We are told Satan rules the Earth and will rule the Earth until Christ returns to take back that which He purchased with His blood. Don't ever let anybody convince you Satan and Jesus are some kind of equals, but opposites. The Bible clearly tells us Jesus Christ, God, *created* Satan.

Satan is called the "ruler of this world" and "the power of darkness." He is a powerful force. His spirit directs leaders, nations, and people. Satan hates the Jews because they brought forth the Messiah and will be instrumental in His return. Satan hates *believing* Christians because they love and worship the Messiah. The Bible warns he will try to destroy both. We are told to beware of wolves among the sheep. He often uses those who *call* themselves Christians or Jews to destroy. This powerful angel is given many names and titles in the Bible . . .

- *Satan* (adversary, *enemy*)   (1 Chr 21:1, Job 1:6, Jn 13:27)
- *Abaddon* (Hebrew: *Destroyer*)   (Rev 9:11)
- *Lucifer* (the shining one, morning star)   (Isa 14:12)
- The *Devil*   (Matt 4:1, Luke 4:2, Luke 4:6)
- The *ruler of the demons*   (Matt 12:24)
- The *god of this age*   (2 Cor 4:4)
- The *ruler of this world*   (Jn 12:31, Jn 14:30, Jn 16:11)
- *Ruler of the darkness of this age*   (Eph 6:12)
- The *anointed cherub who covers*   (Ezek 28:14)
- *Apollyon* (Greek: *Destroyer*)   (Rev 9:11)
- The *father of all lies*   (John 8:44)
- *The liar*   (John 8:44)
- *Lying* spirit   (1 King 22:22)
- The *prince of the power of the air*   (Eph 2:2)
- The *power of darkness*   (Col 1:13)
- *Beelzebub* (Dung-god, lord of the flies)   (Mark 3:22)
- The *wicked one*   (Matt 13:19, Matt 13:38)
- The great *red dragon*   (Rev 12:3)
- The *dragon*   (Rev 12:4,7,13,17,13:2,4,16:13, 20:2)
- The *great dragon*   (Rev 12:9)

- The *murderer* (John 8:44)
- The *accuser* (Rev 12:10)
- The *serpent* (Gen 3:4, Gen 3:14, 2 Cor 11:3)
- That *old serpent* (Rev 12:9, Rev 20:2)
- The *angel of the bottomless pit* (Rev 9:11)
- The *Tempter* (Matt 4:3, 1 Thes 3:5)

God first reveals Satan and his methods in the book of Genesis . . .

"The serpent was more cunning
than any beast of the field which the LORD God had made.
And he [Satan] said to the woman [Eve],
"Has God indeed said, 'You shall not eat
of every tree of the garden'?"
And the woman said to the serpent,
"We may eat the fruit of the trees of the garden;
but of the fruit of the tree which is in the midst of the garden,
God has said, 'You shall not eat it,
nor shall you touch it, lest you die.'"
Then the serpent [Satan] said to the woman,
"You will not surely die."
"For God knows that in the day you eat of it
your eyes will be opened, and you will be like God,
knowing good and evil."
So when the woman saw that the tree was good for food,
that it was pleasant to the eyes,
and a tree desirable to make one wise,
she took of its fruit and ate.
She also gave to her husband with her, and he ate."
    (Gen 3:1-6)

What does God reveal about this creature, Satan, and his tactics in these short verses?

1. *"The serpent was more cunning than any beast of the field which the LORD God had made." And he [Satan] said to the woman, "Has God indeed said, 'You shall not eat of every tree of the garden?'"*

   Satan speaks with authority. He speaks *through* people and leaders. He sounds convincing. Satan knows the Bible and will cast doubt on God's Word and will twist its meaning in attempts to confuse us.

2. *"And the woman [Eve] said to the serpent [Satan],*
   'We may eat the fruit of the trees of the garden;
   but of the fruit of the tree which is in the midst of the garden,'
   God has said, 'You shall not eat it, nor shall you touch it,
   lest you die.'"

   "Then the serpent [Satan] said to the woman,
   'You will not surely die.'"

   Satan is a liar. Speaking lies, convincing lies, with authority, is one of his identifying traits *and of those people his spirit is working through.* One of Satan's great tactics is to first *deny* the truth (quickly countering truth with a strong denial) and then fill the air with false accusations and lies, saying *anything* to turn our attention and focus away from truth. In studying the Bible, we find God hates liars and that He hears each and every lie . . .

3. *And then the serpent said to the woman, "You will surely not die."*

The voice of Satan will oppose and twist the Word of God. The Bible warns that being cast into Hell is the death we should fear. Hell is the death Jesus came to "save" us from. We can also read this seductive lie - "I've been a pretty good person, so I'll go to Heaven," or "*All* religions lead to Heaven," or "Death is a long sleep," or "It's all over when we die," or "Hell is temporary." However, the Bible tells us clearly that each man or woman is given only *one* short life on Earth, and then *after this life* comes the separation and judgement Jesus is trying to save us from . . .

> *"And as it is appointed for men to die once,*
> *but after this the judgment,*
> so Christ was offered once to bear the sins of many.
> To those who eagerly wait for Him
> He will appear a second time,
> apart from sin, for salvation [to save us]." (Heb 9:27-28)

Another of Satan's seductive lies . . . reincarnation. Reincarnation tries to remove or defer the responsibility of the decision each of us must make in this short lifetime. Reincarnation tells us we will have plenty of time and plenty of lives to try to get it right. The Bible teaches us differently, very differently. The Bible tells us we have only one life in which the faith, heart, and spirit, in each man and woman is tested. Then, after this short life, we are each judged and separated. The Bible teaches *there is no second chance.* Either the Bible is right, or those who teach reincarnation, soul sleep, or a temporary purgatory are right. Only one can be right. *You* have to decide. In this one, short life which we are given, we must either sincerely accept and believe in Jesus' payment for our sins on the Cross or we must reject it. Sadly, the utter darkness, loneliness, and torment of Hell will be filled with those who were convinced to reject it and with procrastinators who were convinced to ignore it.

4. *"And then the serpent [Satan] said, 'For God knows that in the day you eat of it your eyes will be opened, and you will be like God, knowing good and evil.'"*

Another of Satan's seductive lies. He entices our egos and pride. The world, through Satan, teaches us to put *self* first and the love of self will bring happiness and fill the loneliness and emptiness found in this life. The Bible teaches just the opposite. The Bible tells us to put *others* first. Jesus says that we, as Christians, are to obey two Commandments. His Commandments are simple:

First, to love God above all else in life. He deserves it. Thank Him for those things which are good, get to know Him through prayer and the Bible, ask Him to help you through those difficult times, hand your fears, anger, and heartbreak over to Him, ask Him to guide your path, show Him respect, obey Him, and have a sense of awe of Him . . .

Second, to love others as ourselves. We are commanded by the Lord to treat all others (even our enemies) just as we would want to be treated in each and every situation. The Bible provides examples of *how* to obey the Lord, such as restraining our angry outbursts, refusing to hurt others, or gossip, steal, curse, or lie. We are told we should not demand to get our own way, envy others, refuse to forgive, refuse to share, or pass by others in their time of need, and we are taught to *strive* to be gentle, kind, and patient. Every one of us will be held accountable. Jesus teaches us to have the heart of a servant. Most of us carry the self-image of a prince or princess, or little god or goddess, continually placing our desires and comfort above others while always scheming to get our own way. Placing our "self" above others is wrong. Jesus has given us only two commandments. To obey these commandments requires strength. This *is* strength. This is contrary to and conflicts with our fallen nature. This requires His strength. Jesus says He will forgive us and help us when we fail.

Satan's fall came from pride, from being puffed up with self importance. We are told God hates pride and a proud look. Satan's tactics of convincing us to love self have not changed, just look at the "Self-help" and "New Age" sections in the bookstore. "Me first," "*My* way," and "Sex, drugs, and rock 'n' roll". . . Satan's power and influence are real.

5.   *"So when the woman saw that the tree was good for food, that it was pleasant to the eyes, and a tree desirable to make one wise, she took of its fruit and ate. She also gave to her husband with her and he ate."*

The allures of this world. Our desires for attention and pleasure are nothing new. The desires Satan throws into our lives to distract us and to destroy us are not scary or frightening, but like fishing lures, *attract* us. He tries to seduce us through our senses. He says, "If it feels good do it." And, as with Eve giving Adam the fruit, he uses people, even those we trust, to draw us into sin. Sadly, the feelings of guilt can often keep us away from the Cross and from Jesus who will lovingly forgive us and remove *all* guilt. God warns the attention, riches, and pleasures we seek in this life are filled with emptiness, and the excitement they seductively offer will quickly vanish like vapor. Like a small child chasing a butterfly into a dark forest, the enticing allures in life can draw us away from God and away from His narrow path of safety . . .

Now, through the prophet Ezekiel, God reveals even more about Satan. This is also an example of why the Bible is so fascinating. The prophet is revealing a prophecy about a real prince, a contemporary ruler living in Tyre (around Lebanon) and then, *seemingly out of nowhere*, the Holy Spirit suddenly shifts gears and switches to a *"king"* of Tyre. As you will soon discover, *this is no ordinary king.* This king was in the Garden of Eden. We only know of four in the Garden - God, Adam, Eve, and Lucifer (Satan). God is not describing Himself, or Adam, or Eve, so, seemingly out of nowhere, God pops in some incredibly *important* detail, insight, and information concerning this powerful and deadly creature, Satan. This is also one of several (mysterious) passages where the Bible reveals to us the force behind an empire, a nation, or even some leaders, is not human, but a dark spiritual force. Another such passage is found in Daniel 10:12, where we find an angel explaining to Daniel that he, the angel, was held up for 21 days while he fought the (spiritual) "prince" of Persia and required Michael, the mighty Archangel, to come and help him. Then, the angel says after leaving Daniel he will have to fight through the (spiritual) "prince" of Greece. So, even though Greece would not become a world power for many, many years *after* Daniel lived and wrote this prophecy, the powerful spiritual force which would direct this empire was apparently already moving into place. In this passage the Holy Spirit redirects the prophet Ezekiel, telling him to prophesy to the spiritual force behind "Tyre." Ezekiel was told to write . . .

"Son of man, take up a lamentation for the king of Tyre,
and say to him, 'Thus says the Lord GOD:
"You were the seal of perfection,
Full of wisdom and perfect in beauty.
You were in Eden, the garden of God;
Every precious stone was your covering:
The sardius, topaz, and diamond, Beryl, onyx,
and jasper, sapphire, turquoise, and emerald with gold.
The workmanship of your timbrels and pipes
Was prepared for you on the day you were created.
"You were the anointed cherub who covers;
I established you; you were on the holy mountain of God;
You walked back and forth in the midst of fiery stones.
You were perfect in your ways from the day you were created,
Till iniquity was found in you.
By the abundance of your trading
You became filled with violence within, and you sinned;
Therefore I cast you as a profane thing
out of the mountain of God;

And I destroyed you, O covering cherub,
From the midst of the fiery stones.
Your heart was lifted up because of your beauty;
You corrupted your wisdom for the sake of your splendor;
I cast you to the ground . . ."
    (Ezek 28:12-17)

In these verses God provides a momentary peek into that dimension which is hidden and shrouded in mystery and darkness. God reveals a little more of that dark creature Satan . . .

1. *"You were the seal of perfection,*
    full of wisdom and perfect in beauty"

    Satan is not ugly. This powerful creature was created
    with great intelligence and beauty.

2. *"You were in Eden, the garden of God; every precious stone was*
    your covering: the sardius, topaz, and diamond, Beryl, onyx, and
    jasper, sapphire, turquoise, and emerald with gold"

    Apparently, while in the Garden of Eden, Lucifer was covered in
    light. Lucifer means "the shining one" or the "morning star." The
    beauty of precious gems is in the light and colors they emit.

3. *"The workmanship of your timbrels and pipes was prepared for*
    you on the day you were created."

    God wants us to know that Satan, or Lucifer, is a created being.

4. *"You were the anointed cherub who covers;"*

    The anointed cherub who covers. *Powerful.* The very top of
    God's creation in heaven.

46

5. *"I established you; you were on the holy mountain of God; you walked back and forth in the midst of fiery stones"*

The "fiery stones" could refer to the stars. We don't really know. God makes it very clear we are *not alone* in the universe. There are at least two other classes of creatures (created beings) described in the Bible. These two other classes of creatures we are told and warned about are called angels and demons. We are warned *never* to call on, or pray to angels. Nowhere does the Bible say these creatures have the same dimensional limitations Man has, or are bound to Earth like Man. Nowhere does it say these creatures could not build a monument on Mars. There are even some who suggest this coming world leader, the Antichrist, might proclaim that he has some kind of an extra-terrestrial origin or connection. As truly bizarre as it sounds, it is probably worth noting. Satan will do anything to cast doubt on or deny God's Word. The world is ready to believe *anything* as long as it takes our eyes and our faith away from the blood on the Cross.

6. *"You were perfect in your ways from the day you were created, till iniquity [sin] was found in you."*

God wants to make it very clear that Satan was *created.*

7. *"By the abundance of your trading [wealth, merchandise] you became filled with violence within, and you sinned; therefore I cast you as a profane thing out of the mountain of God; and I destroyed you, O covering cherub, from the midst of the fiery stones."*

God hates violence and God hates pride. We are told Satan is filled with violence and pride. God will not allow violence or selfish, "puffed-up" pride in His Kingdom. God Himself will cast Satan out of heaven. Sadly, we get hints that God loved or loves Lucifer, as He does all of His creation. God is filled with an infinite amount of love and compassion. In God's time, which can see the end from the beginning, and in God's eyes, Satan, including death, is *already* destroyed. Satan will continue to inflict pain, violence, sickness, heartbreak, loneliness, and death in our lives on Earth until Christ returns. I tremble at the thought of anyone spending their eternity, confined and alone in the vast darkness of Hell with this creature.

8. *"Your heart was lifted up because of your beauty;*
   you corrupted your wisdom for the sake of your splendor;"

We need to beware of idolizing beauty and splendor. How important have we allowed these to become? What does the world worship today? We should take note. It is interesting to watch the world's frenzy and worship of beauty and splendor as we get closer to "that Day." Watch, as "the world" of Hollywood, fashion, music, print, and television continues to cleave together, forming, creating, and worshiping the image, the creature, while lifting up their "gods" and "goddesses." It is sad to see how quickly the darkness of "the world" lures, ensnares, corrupts, and destroys those it attracts and raises up. Beware. We are warned this powerful angel Satan, called the *"ruler of this world,"* will continue to rule over the world until Christ returns.

God looks into our hearts. Real beauty in God's eyes is the humble and meek spirit that bears the fruit of patience, gentleness, forgiveness, kindness, thanksgiving, gratitude, and self-control, with a fear, awe, respect, and love for God. One who appreciates the Lord's kindness, His love, His compassion, His patience, His forgiveness, and the deep mercies of His Grace.

9. *"I cast you to the ground . . ."*

We are told that Satan, the great Red Dragon, will be cast out of heaven and down to Earth. He will draw a third of the angels with him.

"I cast you out, for I never knew you . . ."

Many will hear those chilling words as they stand before the Lord Jesus. Jesus now stands at the door and knocks. Most will refuse to open that door to invite Him into their lives to help, to strengthen, to comfort, and to heal. He lovingly wraps His arms around the lonely and the brokenhearted. Jesus will never cast away or turn away any man or woman that willingly comes to Him, regardless of how young or how old, or how good or how bad. Any and all who come to Him with a sincere and humbled heart are welcomed with open arms. *Each of us will be tested.* Only Jesus Christ can, and will, offer you a new life, even now.

Through the prophet Isaiah, God reveals more about Satan . . .

"How you are fallen from heaven, O Lucifer, son of the morning!
How you are cut down to the ground,
you who weakened the nations!
For you have said in your heart:
'*I will* ascend into heaven,
I will exalt my throne above the stars of God;
I will also sit on the mount of the congregation
on the farthest sides of the north;
I will ascend above the heights of the clouds,
I will be like the Most High [God].'
Yet you shall be brought down to Sheol [Hell],
to the lowest depths of the Pit."   (Isa 14:12-15)

The five "*I wills*" of Satan. *I, me, mine, myself!!!* The *spirit* of Satan. We are *all* born with it and only the Spirit of God, through love and discipline, can remove it from us. This great Red Dragon, filled with unspeakable violence and evil, will be cast down to Earth . . .

"And another sign appeared in heaven:
behold, a great, fiery red dragon [Satan]
having seven heads and ten horns,
and seven diadems on his heads.
His tail drew a third of the stars [angels] of heaven
and threw them to the earth." (Rev 12:3-4)

"So the great dragon was cast out, that serpent of old,
called the Devil and Satan, who deceives the whole world;
he was cast to the Earth,
and his angels were cast out with him." (Rev 12:9)

"For we do not wrestle against flesh and blood,
but against principalities, against powers,
against the rulers of the darkness of this age,
against spiritual hosts of wickedness in the heavenly places."
[these are ranks of angels and demons] (Eph 6:12)

Satan and his angels, the fallen ones, apparently *one-third* of all angels created, will be cast down to Earth. Before this they roamed both heaven and Earth. Satan and most of his angels are not currently confined in Hell. When Satan is cast down to Earth he will no longer have access to God or Heaven. We are told the Earth is already a spiritual battlefield. The final battle will be fought on Earth. Many think it will start very soon. We can already feel the heat and stench of Satan's foul breath as we look at the violence, lies, war, and disease spreading across the Earth.

"Choose this day whom you will serve . . . "

Jesus warns, *"He who is not with Me is against Me."*
[You are either for Him or against Him . . .]
(Matt 12:30)

"And if it seems evil to you to serve the LORD,
choose for yourselves this day whom you will serve."
(Joshua 24:15)

Each person on Earth must choose whom they will serve. The Bible says the choice is clear. Jesus says we are either for Him or against Him. We are either His friend or His enemy. There is no in between. There is no neutral ground. To simply ignore the choice *is* a choice. We are warned the final battle will be fought soon. "For we do not wrestle against flesh and blood." It is a spiritual battle. Those who serve Christ are behind "enemy lines" until He returns. Persevere. Pray for God's help in understanding the Bible. This will help to guard against the many subtle attacks against our faith. Be cautious. "Read between the lines" and take a little time to consider those things which are now being offered to entertain us. Satan will use any tool and weapon he can to imitate, ridicule, or confuse the Word of God to weaken our belief. What Satan offers as substitutes to take our eyes and faith off of the Cross can be very pleasant to the eyes and ears. Hold fast in faith and in courage. Beware. Jesus says the world that hated Him will also hate those who follow Him. It will not be easy. He will return, as promised, in power and glory. Rewards are promised for all those who wait in faith.

The Beast: The rise of Satan's Antichrist . . .

The world will soon get the leader it seems to be longing and waiting for. A powerful leader who will be popular, attractive, charismatic, and a great talker whose many words will not be chosen for truth, but for deception. A leader who will kill many Christians . . .

> "Then I stood on the sand of the sea.
> And I saw a beast [Satan's Antichrist]
> rising up out of the sea,
> having seven heads and ten horns,
> and on his horns ten crowns,
> [other prophecies tell us these represent nations in Europe]
> and on his heads a blasphemous name . . .
> *The dragon (Satan) gave him his power,*
> *his throne, and great authority.*" *(*Rev 13:1,2)

> "The coming of the lawless one [the Antichrist]
> *is according to the working of Satan,*
> *with all power, signs [miracles], and lying wonders*"
>   (II Th 2:9-10)

> "It was granted to him to make war with the saints
> and to overcome them [he will slaughter millions].
> *And authority was given him*
> *over every tribe, tongue, and nation.*" (Rev 13:7)
> [This coming dictator *will* rule the "One-World" Government]

> "Woe to the worthless shepherd,
> who leaves the flock! [Israel . . . Jewish?]
> *A sword shall be against his arm and against his right eye;*
> *his [the Antichrist's] arm shall completely wither,*
> *and his right eye shall be totally blinded.*" (Zech 11:17)
> [This may happen when he receives his mortal "head" wound]

This man whom we call the Antichrist has been given many different titles in the Bible. The term "Antichrist" is unfortunate, because it is misleading. Misleading in that although this man will be against Christ, the world will see him as a "*pseudo*-christ." This future world leader will be Satan's *counterfeit* Christ. This world leader will be very, very popular in the eyes of the world. The world will view him as a great leader and as a messiah. God sees this man as a vicious and bloodthirsty "*Beast.*"

We are told quite a bit about this future world leader, Satan's counterfeit messiah, who will someday soon rise to power . . .

- He will be indwelt and empowered by Satan.
- He will rise to power over Europe and then over the world.
- He will bring peace, yet conquer through treaties and war.
- He will be very, very popular around the world.
- He will be a great talker and speech maker.
- He will likely be charismatic and attractive, like King Saul.
- He will receive what appears to be a fatal wound to the head.
- He will appear to be resurrected from the dead.
- His right eye may be blinded and his arm completely withered.
- He will enforce a 7 year treaty with Israel.
  [It doesn't say he *signs* this treaty, but he *enforces* some treaty]
- He may help to get the new Jewish Temple built in Jerusalem.
- He will require that everybody on Earth receive some kind of mark or identification on their forehead or hand and nobody will be able to buy or sell without it.
- He will stand in a new Jewish Temple in Jerusalem and declare that he is "God" (Probably will be televised).
- Terror will reign on Earth for *exactly* 3½ years after this event.
- He will direct the slaughter of millions of Christians and Jews.
- He will lead the armies of the world into Armageddon . . .

A Second Beast will Rise.
The Antichrist will have a religious partner . . .

> "Then I saw *another* beast coming up out of the Earth,
> and he had *two horns like a lamb*
> and *spoke like a dragon*.
> And he exercises all the authority
> of the first beast [the Antichrist] in his presence,
> and causes the Earth and those who dwell in it
> to worship the first beast [the Antichrist],
> whose deadly [head] wound was healed."   (Rev 13:11-12)

The Antichrist will not be alone. Another man, also empowered by Satan, will rule alongside the Antichrist. This powerful and deadly *religious* leader or "beast" (as God sees him) will rise to world power with the Antichrist. In this prophecy God reveals some important information and details concerning this religious man of power . . .

"Two horns like a lamb," tells us he will emerge with Christian credentials or doctrine, but *"spoke like a dragon"* tells us he will be controlled and directed by Satan. There are hints this man *might* even be Jewish. This person, along with the religious system he will lead, is also referred to as *"The Woman Who Rides the Beast."* We are warned this all encompassing, one-world religion will rise to power out of Rome.

The "Image of the Beast" . . .

> "He was granted power to give breath to the image of the beast,
> that the image of the beast should both speak and cause as many
> as would not worship the image of the beast to be killed."
> (Rev 13:15)

This religious leader will create some sort of an "image" representing the Antichrist. It may be something very miraculous, or it may be two-thousand year old vocabulary trying to describe some future technology such as robotics, animatronics, or virtual reality.

The "Mark of the Beast"...

"He causes *all*, both small and great, rich and poor, free and slave,
to receive a mark on their right hand or on their foreheads,
and that *no one may buy or sell except one who has the mark,
or the name of the beast, or the number of his name."*
(Rev 13:16-17)

This prophecy is very crucial for those who have not accepted Jesus Christ as their Lord and will be alive when this law is enacted and enforced. This "mark" may be some kind of tatoo, or implanted microchip with all of your credit card and banking information, we really don't know right now. It will not be easy to refuse this mark, whatever it is, for many of you will have families and children that will need to be fed. *By taking this mark, you will have sealed your eternal fate and doom.* In God's eyes it identifies *you* with the Antichrist. There will be no turning back for any who take the "mark, the name of the beast, or the number of his name."

An enigma...

"Here is wisdom.
Let him who has understanding
calculate the number of the beast [the Antichrist],
for it is the number of a man:
His number is 666."
(Rev 13:18)

55

APOCALYPSE

THE VIOLENT END

" The Day of the Lord . . .

That day is a day of wrath,

A day of trouble and distress,

A day of devastation and desolation,

A day of darkness and gloominess,

A day of clouds and thick darkness,

A day of trumpet and alarm . . . "

Zeph 1:14, 15

The Trumpet Sounds . . .

*A*s God looks down upon the Earth He sees the violence. He sees the gross and rampant immorality and how casually we accept it. He feels the rebellion. He hears each lie. He hears the blasphemies spoken in earnest and in jest against His name and the name of His Son, whom He sent forth from Heaven. He knows what is about to happen. Yet, as He looks upon us, it is with a heart filled with love and compassion. A heart willing to forgive and forget. A heart that yearns for His children to come to repentance (to change), and return to Him. He sent forth His prophets to reason with and to warn the people. But His prophets were brutally beaten, imprisoned, and murdered. Then He sent forth His Son . . . not to judge the sinner, but to save the sinner. And through His Son He extends an offer. An offer to save each of us from the *second* death (the torment of Hell) *and* to hide and shelter those who are waiting in faith from the great and awesome "Day of the Lord." Jesus came to show us the Way. But, as with Jeremiah, Elijah, Zechariah, Isaiah, and other prophets sent before Him who were imprisoned, beaten, and killed, the political and religious rulers of the day *once again* treated a prophet of God with arrogance, envy, malice, and evil intent. They had Him tortured, then put to death. Only this time it was different. Not just a prophet, but He *Himself* who stepped forth from Eternity to take on the form of man . . . as the son of Man . . . the Son of God. This time, a living sacrifice for all of mankind, once and for all. Taking upon Himself the punishment and penalty due to each of us for all sin. The only burden He asks us to carry is simply the burden of accepting *or* rejecting His offer. "The foolishness of the Cross." He hated it and despised the shame. Yet, He endured it as He hung there in pain and agony, nailed to that cross of wood, out of love. His love for you and for me. *Just as the prophets had said He would.*

Right now He stands at the door and knocks. It is our responsibility to open that door and invite Him into our lives. Right now He stands with open arms willing to receive any and all who will come to Him. He will turn no one away, regardless how young or how old, regardless of the sins they have committed. Today He waits patiently seated on His throne in Heaven. Waiting while His offer of grace is extended to all peoples and nations on Earth. Sent first to the people of Abraham, Isaac, and Jacob, and then to *all* nations, to *all* peoples. He has fulfilled His Abrahamic Covenant. There is a day, we are told, when His patience will end. He will shut the door. He warns that His Covenant of Grace will not last forever. It will be replaced with a Covenant of Justice . . .

These events which are about to be unleashed on this world, even though global in nature, appear to focus on one thing - the tiny nation of Israel. One tiny piece of land. A speck of land when compared to the massive, rich, and powerful enemies that surround her on all sides (look at a map). A land God calls His own. God says He owns it and the sons and daughters of Israel are His. The Bible says the children of Israel will be punished for profaning God's Holy Name while dispersed among the nations (Ezek. 36:17-29). The Bible warns the rest of the world will not go unpunished and also warns the enemies of Israel are the enemies of God . . .

"Cursed be everyone who curses you [Israel],
and blessed be those who bless you!"
(Gen 27:29)

The situation in Israel and the Middle East will continue to grow worse and worse. *Watch your television. There will be no peace in Israel until the Messiah, Jesus Christ, returns.* Don't be seduced into believing the political rhetoric and deceptions coming out of your television concerning "peace settlements" or Israel's enemies willing to trade "land for peace." Know this, that through the shrieking and howling of the enemies of Israel and their empty promises, it is not the size of Israel they fear, but it is the *existence* of Israel. Her enemies (including many of our national leaders) will try to coerce her with promises, they will threaten her, they will attack her, Russia and allies are going to invade her, the coming world leader who will soon rise over Europe (the Antichrist) will seduce her with promises and treaties, all of the nations of the world will turn against her, and the armies of the world will someday gather against her at Armageddon to strike her with a final death blow.

Watch, as the power of Satan continues to incite Israel's enemies, the enemies of God . . .

And listen, as the shrill and angry voices of Satan continue to harden the hearts and minds of people around the world against Israel *and* against Jesus Christ, the Messiah, thus losing their only hope.

There is a crushing weight associated with the words found in this section. We are told we live in an age of darkness mixed with light. Jesus calls those who believe in Him and wait in faith, the "salt of the Earth." Salt is a preservative. We are told those who sincerely believe in Him and wait in faith are filled with "light." Satan is called the "prince of darkness" and the "ruler of this world." The world hates the light, for as a light shining into a dark place, the light reveals those things we do which are not right. The light acts as a *restraining* force. Jesus will someday return as a "thief in the night" to remove the children of light, in a moment, "in the twinkling of an eye," to protect and shelter them from those things which are about to come

upon a violent, arrogant, and unbelieving world. A world in opposition to God. There is the promise of Light returning *after* these things take place. The purpose of prophecy is to authenticate God's word and to prepare those who wait in faith. God takes no delight in these things. It is His hope that all will change their ways and return to Him, through His Son, so that *all* might escape these things that are about to come upon the Earth. We are told Noah was a preacher of righteousness and for 120 years was God's witness, a trumpet of warning, while he built the vessel of refuge and escape. There could have been a billion people living on Earth at the time of Noah. They were eating, drinking, marrying, and giving in marriage. People on Earth were feeling content without God. The Earth was filled with violence. People ignored and disobeyed God's laws and simply *did that which was right in their own eyes*. After 120 years of waiting and warning, God Himself closed the door to the Ark . . .
Eight people were saved.

The Day is real and the hour is set.

The coming Apocalypse . . .

THE PROPHECIES

"When I heard, my belly trembled;
my lips quivered at the voice:
rottenness entered into my bones,
and I trembled in myself,
that I might rest [escape]
in the Day of trouble."
(Hab 3:16)

The Antichrist will rise and conquer...

"Now I saw when the Lamb opened one of the seals;
and I heard one of the four living creatures
saying with a voice like thunder, 'Come and see.'
And I looked, and behold, a white horse.
And he who sat on it had a bow;
and a crown was given to him,
and he went out conquering and to conquer." (Rev 6:1-2)
[The Antichrist will be Satan's *counterfeit* Messiah]

A Great War will ignite the Earth...

"When He opened the second seal,
I heard the second living creature saying,
'Come and see.'
Another horse, fiery red, went out.
And it was granted to the one who sat on it
to take peace from the Earth,
and that people should kill one another;
and there was given to him a great sword." (Rev 6:3-4)

Global famine, severe food shortages will follow . . .

"When He opened the third seal,
I heard the third living creature say,
'Come and see.'
So I looked, and behold, a black horse,
and he who sat on it had a pair of scales in his hand.
And I heard a voice in the midst of the four living creatures
saying, "A quart of wheat for a denarius,
[A denarius was equal to about a *full day's* wage]
and three quarts of barley for a denarius;
and do not harm the oil and the wine."
[The rulers will still have their luxuries]   (Rev 6:5-6)

One-fourth of all people will be quickly destroyed . . .

"When He opened the fourth seal,
I heard the voice of the fourth living creature saying,
'Come and see.'
And I looked, and behold, a pale horse.
And the name of him who sat on it was Death,
and Hades followed with him.
And power was given to them over a fourth of the Earth,
to kill with sword, with hunger, with death,
and by the beasts of the Earth."   (Rev 6:7-8)
[These "beasts" may be military, political, and religious rulers.]

A massive nuclear missile attack or meteor storm will cause the Earth to convulse under its deadly power . . .

It is interesting to note that those nations which are now armed with large arsenals of nuclear weapons have already built and are continuing to build massive "emergency command centers" into and under mountains to hide their leaders in case of all out nuclear war.

> "And the stars of heaven fell to the Earth,
> as a fig tree drops its late figs
> when it is shaken by a mighty wind.
> Then the sky receded as a scroll when it is rolled up,
> and every mountain and island was moved out of its place
> *And the kings of the Earth, the great men, the rich men,*
> the commanders, the mighty men, every slave and every free man,
> *hid themselves in the caves and in the rocks of the mountains"*
> (Rev 6:13-15)

One-third of all trees on Earth will burn . . .

After the nuclear bomb tests in the Pacific, the Navy discovered much of the massive damage to the target fleet was caused by giant hail stones which were generated by the nuclear blasts. If the nuclear blasts had been over a large city, much blood would have been drawn up into the cloud and mingled with the hail . . .

> "The first angel sounded:
> *And hail and fire followed, mingled with blood,*
> and they were thrown to the Earth.
> *And a third of the trees were burned up,*
> and all green grass was burned up." (Rev 8:7)

66

Nuclear missiles or a large asteroid will destroy one-third of all life in the sea . . .

"Then the second angel sounded:
And something like a great mountain burning with fire
was thrown into the sea, and a third of the sea became blood.
And a third of the living creatures in the sea died,
and a third of the ships were destroyed."
   (Rev 8:8-9)

A massive nuclear warhead or an asteroid will strike and poison one-third of all fresh water on Earth . . .

In old Russian Bibles the word "Wormwood" was translated, *Chernobyl!*

"Then the third angel sounded:
And a great star fell from heaven, burning like a torch,
and it fell on a third of the rivers and on the springs of water;
And the name of the star is Wormwood [bitter].
a third of the waters became wormwood,
and many men died from the water, because it was made bitter."
   (Rev 8:10-11)

Nuclear winter?
Smoke and ash will block one-third of the light . . .

"Then the fourth angel sounded:
And a third of the sun was struck,
a third of the moon, and a third of the stars,
so that a third of them were darkened;
And a third of the day did not shine,

and likewise the night.
And I looked, and I heard an angel
flying through the midst of heaven,
saying with a loud voice,
"Woe, woe, woe to the inhabitants of the Earth,
because of the remaining blasts of the trumpet
of the three angels who are about to sound!"
    (Rev 8:12-13)

One-third of the remaining population on Earth will then be destroyed . . .

The Bible tells us only a small remnant of the population on Earth will survive the Apocalypse.   Although, here, we find angels being released, much of the global terror will come from *mankind* destroying *mankind*, nation destroying nation, deadly wave after deadly wave. The Holy Spirit goes out of his way to let us know that the day and the hour is real and has already been set. Remember, *our future is already history . . .*

"Then the sixth angel sounded: And I heard a voice
from the four horns of the golden altar which is before God,
saying to the sixth angel who had the trumpet,
"Release the four angels who are bound
at the great river Euphrates."
So the four angels, who had been prepared
for the hour and day and month and year,
were released to kill a third of mankind."
    (Rev 9:13-15)

A 200,000,000 man army will rise using weapons of mass destruction to kill yet another one-third of mankind . . .

This prophecy says the "army *of* the horsemen was two hundred million." These "horsemen" may be a small division or group within that army, such as a strategic nuclear weapons division, or they may be brightly painted missiles sitting upon missile launchers. The "two hundred million" is to help identify the nation or area they will rise out of. Later called "the kings of the East," it appears the Chinese military *is* someday going to use the secret missile technology our leader(s) sold them - *against us!* One-third of mankind will be killed . . .

"Now the number of the army of the horsemen
was two hundred million;
[For the first time ever such an army could be raised in China]
I heard the number of them.
And thus I saw the horses in the vision:
those who sat on them had breastplates of fiery red,
hyacinth blue, and sulfur yellow; and the heads of the horses
were like the heads of lions; and out of their mouths came fire,
smoke, and brimstone [sulfur, or a kind of poisoned air].
By these three plagues a third of mankind was killed--
by the fire and the smoke and the brimstone
which came out of their mouths.
For their power is in their mouth and in their tails;
for their tails are like serpents, having heads;
and with them they do harm." (Rev 9:16-19*)*

Every living creature left in the sea will die . . .

"Then the second angel poured out his bowl on the sea,
and it became blood as of a dead man;
and every living creature in the sea died." (Rev 16:3)

69

Rivers and springs will turn to blood . . .

God tells us *why* they will turn to blood.

> "Then the third angel poured out his bowl
> on the rivers and springs of water, and they became blood.
> And I heard the angel of the waters saying:
> "You are righteous, O Lord,
> the One who is and who was and who is to be,
> because You have judged these things.
> *For they have shed the blood of saints and prophets,*
> *and You have given them blood to drink.*
> *For it is their just due."*
>   (Rev 16:4-7)

A great heat will scorch the Earth . . .

People on Earth will continue to curse God . . .

> "Then the fourth angel poured out his bowl on the sun,
> and power was given to him to scorch men with fire.
> And men were scorched with great heat,
> and they blasphemed the name of God
> who has power over these plagues;
> and they did not repent and give Him glory.
>   (Rev 16:8-9)

A thick, darkness will cover the Earth . . .

People on Earth will gnaw their tongues in pain and agony and will continue to curse God . . .

> "Then the fifth angel poured out his bowl
> on the throne of the beast,
> and his kingdom became full of darkness;
> and they gnawed their tongues because of the pain.
> They blasphemed the God of heaven
> because of their pains and their sores,
> and did not repent of their deeds."
> (Rev 16:10-11)

Millions who come to the Lord will be executed . . .

God will take the sting out of death for the millions who will die in faith, and wants them to know they will be blessed in Heaven . . .

> Then I heard a voice from heaven saying to me,
> "Write: *'Blessed are the dead who die in the Lord from now on.'"*
> "Yes," says the Spirit, *"that they may rest from their labors,*
> *and their works follow them."*
> (Rev 14:13)

> *"Then I saw the souls of those who had been beheaded*
> for their witness to Jesus and for the word of God,
> who had not worshiped the beast [the Antichrist]
> or his image, and had not received his mark
> on their foreheads or on their hands."
> (Rev 20:4)

There are millions of Christians today in China, Iran, Saudi Arabia, Sudan, Indonesia, Algeria, Egypt, India, and around the world, including women and children, who are being imprisoned, murdered, tortured, raped, beaten, kidnaped, beheaded, burned alive, and sold into slavery simply for their faith in Jesus Christ, while we, our churches, the leaders of our nation, and the news networks simply watch and do nothing . . .

"I saw under the altar the souls of those who had been slain
for the word of God and for the testimony which they held.
And they cried with a loud voice, saying,
"How long, O Lord, holy and true,
until You judge and avenge our blood
on those who dwell on the Earth?"
Then a white robe was given to each of them;
and it was said to them that they should rest a little while longer,
until both the number of their fellow servants and their brethren,
who would be killed as they were, was completed."
    (Rev 6:9-11)

"Now brother will betray brother to death,
and a father his child;
and children will rise up against parents
and cause them to be put to death.
"And you will be hated by all men for My name's [Jesus'] sake.
But he who endures to the end shall be saved."
    (Mark 13:12-13)

A deadly, supernatural hailstorm will strike the Earth . . .

> *"And great hail from heaven fell upon men,*
> *each hailstone* about the weight of a talent.
> [A talent = *85 - 114 pounds!*]
> And men blasphemed God
> because of the plague of the hail,
> since that plague was exceedingly great."
>   (Rev 16:21)

God gave us an earlier hint concerning this judgment of hail way back in the Book of Job, which many believe is the oldest book in the Bible.

> *"And God said,*
> 'Have you seen the treasury of hail,
> *which I have reserved for the time of trouble,*
> *for the day of battle and war?'"*
>   (Job 38:22-23)

Armageddon . . .

"Then the sixth angel poured out his bowl
on the great river Euphrates, and its water was dried up,
so that the way of the kings from the East
might be prepared.
And I saw three unclean spirits like frogs
coming out of the mouth of the dragon, [Satan]
out of the mouth of the beast [the Antichrist],
and out of the mouth of the false prophet. [the *second* Beast]
For they are spirits of demons, performing signs,
which go out to the kings of the Earth and of the whole world,
to gather them to the battle of that great Day of God Almighty ...
And they gathered them together
to the place called in Hebrew, **Armageddon.***"*
  (Rev 16:12-16)

The weapons *will* be used. Much of the world will be destroyed. Cities will disappear. Armageddon means the "Hill of Megiddo." Megiddo is part of the Plain of Esdraelon which is located in central Israel. Napoleon came through there and declared it to be the finest battlefield in the world. The whole world will be drawn into this war over Israel and Jerusalem. No nation will be spared. The Bible warns there will be *three* deadly waves associated with this conflict, including: A Russian lead invasion of Israel, a massive Chinese invasion of the Middle East, which will then be "joined" as the armies of the Antichrist march out of Europe and around the world to the place called "Armageddon." Jesus will return to engage this final battle Himself. He alone will destroy the enemies of Israel. We don't know the time *between* events. We do know that God has set aside *seven years* to complete His plan with Israel, and this Age.

From the *apparent* absence of America in prophecy, it appears the U.S. may be "neutralized" sometime *before* this Middle-East conflict begins. Israel must stand alone . . . Her only hope will be in God.

Listen for a moment, as other prophets cry out their warnings against this coming global battle for Jerusalem which will consume the World in its deadly fire . . .

The prophet Isaiah writes:

"Therefore the anger of the LORD
is aroused against His people [Israel];
[We are told this is for profaning His Holy Name while
they were dispersed among the nations. See "The Warnings"]
He has stretched out His hand against them
and stricken them, and the hills trembled.
Their carcasses were as refuse in the midst of the streets.
For all this His anger is not turned away,
but His hand is stretched out still.
He will lift up a banner to the nations from afar,
and will whistle to them from the end of the Earth;
surely they shall come with speed, swiftly.
No one will be weary or stumble among them,
no one will slumber or sleep;
nor will the belt on their loins be loosed,
nor the strap of their sandals be broken;
Whose arrows are sharp, and all their bows bent;
their horses' hooves will seem like flint,
and their wheels like a whirlwind.
Their roaring will be like a lion, they will roar like young lions;
yes, they will roar and lay hold of the prey;
they will carry it away safely, and no one will deliver.
In that Day [the Day of the Lord]
they will roar against them like the roaring of the sea.
And if one looks to the land, behold, darkness and sorrow;
and the light is darkened by the clouds." (Isa 5:25-30)

The prophet Ezekiel writes:

"Now the word of the LORD came to me, saying, '*Son of man,
set your face against Gog, of the land of Magog [Russia!]*,
the prince of Rosh, Meshech, and Tubal,
and *prophesy against him*, and say, Thus says the Lord GOD:
'Behold, I am against you, O Gog [a coming Russian leader],
the prince of Rosh, Meshech, and Tubal.
I will turn you around, put hooks into your jaws [perhaps a treaty],
and lead you out, with all your army, horses, and horsemen,
all splendidly clothed, a great company with bucklers and shields,
all of them handling swords. [Russia will soon march again . . .]
Persia [Iran], Ethiopia, and Libya [Islamic allies] are with them,
all of them with shield and helmet. Gomer and all its troops; the
house of Togarmah from the far north and all its troops -- many
people are with you. [Russia will also be joined by some Eastern
European forces . . . it appears even Turkey will aid the invasion]
Prepare yourself and be ready, you and all your companies
that are gathered about you; and be a guard for them.
After many days you will be visited. [Meaning, this *is* prophetic]
*In the latter years you [Russia] will come into the land of those
brought back from the sword and gathered from many people on
the mountains of Israel, which had long been desolate;
they [Israel] were brought out of the nations,
and now all of them [nations] dwell safely.*
You will ascend, coming like a storm, covering the land [Israel]
like a cloud, you and all your troops and many peoples with you."
(Ezek 38:1-10)

GOD warns Iran (Persia), with Russia (Magog), and a coalition of
allies (including Turkey, Libya, Sudan) will go to war and will invade
Israel. In Ezekiel 38-39 the Bible warns this coming war between Iran
(Persia) and Israel will take place sometime *after* Israel has been
re-gathered into Her land as a nation (which was fulfilled on May 14,
1948) ... *this prophetic war has never yet taken place* ... the only time

in history Persia (Iran) has ever gone to war against Israel was to help Israel throw off the yoke of the Byzantine Empire around 614 AD.

This will be unlike any other war in history ... this war will unleash a series of *irreversible* events which will change the world *forever*. God has set aside two whole chapters in the Bible to warn Mankind of this coming war ...

We are not exactly sure when *this* invasion will take place. The invading armies will be utterly destroyed . . . by *God*. Verse 39 goes on to hint this battle may involve nuclear weapons because - Israel waits months to enter the battlefield *after* the battle, "professionals" bury the dead, and later if a bone is spotted it is to be "marked" for a professional to bury . . . the aftermath will be very, very gruesome.

The Bible warns the US will NOT defend Israel. According to the Bible, Israel must stand alone ... with God. For when this coming war does finally start, the United States will be unwilling (or unable) to help Israel defend herself. Bible scholars are divided as to whether this coming war is part of the prophetic battle of Armageddon or will just precede Armageddon in order to prepare a path for the Antichrist.

In Ezekiel 39 the Bible goes on to warn the invading armies will be utterly destroyed ... by GOD! Also in Ezekiel 39 there are hints this coming war may go nuclear because Israel will wait months to enter the battlefield after the battle, they will "set apart men regularly employed" (professionals) to bury the dead, and later if a bone is spotted it is to be "marked" for the professionals to bury (exactly the same procedures that are now found in our military nuclear/biological/chemical "battlefield cleanup" manuals today) ... the aftermath of this invasion will be very, very gruesome.

ALL Mankind should be sitting on the edge of their seats with white knuckles watching this terrible prophecy slowly start to unfold ...

The prophet Joel writes:

"Blow the trumpet in Zion [Israel],
and sound an alarm in My holy mountain!
Let all the inhabitants of the land tremble;
for the Day of the LORD is coming, for it is at hand:
A day of darkness and gloominess,
a day of clouds and thick darkness,
like the morning clouds spread over the mountains.
A people come, great and strong [the armies of the Antichrist], the
like of whom has never been; nor will there ever be any such after
them, even for many successive generations.
[This *final* Battle may build sometime *after* the Russian attack]
A fire devours before them, and behind them a flame burns . . .
Every one marches in his own column. [A *disciplined* army]
Though they lunge between the weapons, they are not cut down.
They run to and fro in the city, they run on the wall;
they climb into the houses, they enter at the windows like a thief.
The Earth quakes before them, [Tank battalions?]
the heavens tremble; [Helicopters, bombers, and jet fighters?]
the sun and moon grow dark,
and the stars diminish their brightness." [*Smoke* will fill the air]
        (Joel 2:1-10)

"And I will show wonders in the heavens and in the earth:
blood and fire *and pillars of smoke* [mushroom clouds?].
The sun shall be turned into darkness,
and the moon into blood, [thick smoke can cause this effect]
before the coming of the great and awesome day of the LORD.
And it shall come to pass that whoever calls on the name of the
LORD shall be saved." [I hope many will remember this verse]
        (Joel 2:30-32)

The prophet Jeremiah writes:

"For thus says the LORD God of Israel to me:
'Take this wine cup of fury from My hand,
and cause all the nations, to whom I send you, to drink it.
And they will drink and stagger and go mad
because of the sword that I will send among them.'"
Then I took the cup from the LORD'S hand,
and made all the nations drink, to whom the LORD had sent me:
"Therefore you shall say to them,
'Thus says the LORD of hosts, the God of Israel:
"Drink, be drunk, and vomit!
Fall and rise no more,
because of the sword which I will send among you."'
"And it shall be, if they refuse to take the cup
from your hand to drink, then you shall say to them,
'Thus says the LORD of hosts: "You shall certainly drink!"
"For behold, I begin to bring calamity on the city
which is called by My name [Jerusalem],
and should you [the nations of the world] *be utterly unpunished?*
You shall *not* be unpunished,
for I will call for a sword on *all* the inhabitants of the Earth,"
 says the LORD of hosts.
"Therefore prophesy against them
all these words, and say to them:
'The LORD will roar from on high,
and utter His voice from His holy habitation;
he will roar mightily against His fold. [Israel]

He will give a shout, as those who tread the grapes,
against all the inhabitants of the Earth [against the whole world].
A noise will come to the ends of the Earth . . ."

"Thus says the LORD of hosts:
'Behold, disaster shall go forth from nation to nation,
and a great whirlwind shall be raised up
from the farthest parts of the Earth.
And at that day the slain of the LORD
shall be from one end of the Earth
even to the other end of the Earth.
They shall not be lamented, or gathered, or buried;
they shall become refuse on the ground.
Wail, shepherds, and cry!   [Jewish leaders]
Roll about in the ashes, you leaders of the flock! [Israel]
For the days of your slaughter
and your dispersions are fulfilled;
you shall fall like a precious vessel.
And the shepherds will have no way to flee,
nor the leaders of the flock to escape.
A voice of the cry of the shepherds,
and a wailing of the leaders to the flock will be heard.
For the LORD has plundered their pasture,
And the peaceful dwellings are cut down
because of the fierce anger of the LORD.
He has left His lair like the lion; for their land is desolate
because of the fierceness of the Oppressor,
and because of His [God's] fierce anger.'"
    (Jer 25:15-17, 27-38)

The prophet Zechariah writes:

"For I will gather all the nations to battle against Jerusalem;
the city [Jerusalem] shall be taken,
the houses rifled,
and the women ravished [brutally raped].
Half of the city shall go into captivity,
but the remnant of the people
shall not be cut off from the city. "
    (Zech 14:2)

The LORD, Jesus Christ, will hear His people . . .

"And it shall come to pass in all the land [Israel], says the LORD,
That two-thirds in it shall be cut off and die,
but one-third shall be left in it:
[only ⅓ in Israel will be spared by God - even fewer in the world]
I will bring the one-third through the fire,
will refine them as silver is refined,
and test them as gold is tested.
They will call on My name,
and I will answer them.
I will say, 'This is My people';
and each one will say, 'The LORD is my God.'"
    (Zech 13:8-9)

A massive Earthquake unlike any other in the history of mankind will then convulse and change the Earth . . .

"And there was a great earthquake,
such a mighty and great earthquake
as had not occurred since men were on the earth.
Now the great city [Jerusalem]
was divided into three parts,
and the cities of the nations fell . . .
Then every island fled away,
and the mountains were not found."
　　(Rev 16:18-20)

"The Earth is violently broken,
the Earth is split open,
the Earth is shaken exceedingly.
The Earth shall reel to and fro like a drunkard,
and shall totter like a hut;
its transgression shall be heavy upon it,
and it will fall, and not rise again."
　　(Isa 24:19-20)

. . . as Jesus Christ returns to Earth in awesome power.

"And *in that day*
His feet [the Messiah] will stand
on the Mount of Olives,
which faces Jerusalem on the east.
And the Mount of Olives shall be split in two
from east to west, making a very large valley . . ."
　　(Zech 14:4, 6, 7)

As we will find later, many other prophets wrote of His return . . .

*God has set aside exactly 7 years for much to happen.
As we have seen, the last 3½ of these years
will change the world . . . forever.*

These events will happen quickly and unexpectedly. The world will be taken by surprise. The people of the world will be so caught up with the cares of this life that most will never bother reading the Book (the Bible) or pay attention to the detailed warnings it contains . . .

This section contains only a small sampling of the prophecies and warnings found in the Bible concerning the terrifying events which will someday soon strike and engulf the Earth. God does not wish that *any* should go through this Apocalypse and offers an escape and shelter to all who will draw close to Him, through His Son, Jesus Christ, before the coming time of trouble. Someday it will be too late to consider His offer.

God leaves us with an ominous warning . . .

"Search from the book of the LORD, and read:
not one of these [prophecies] shall fail;
not one shall lack her mate.
For My mouth has commanded it,
and His Spirit has gathered them."
    (Isa 34:16)

"Indeed I have spoken it;
I will also bring it to pass.
I have purposed it;
I will also do it.
Listen to Me, you stubborn-hearted,
who are far from righteousness . . ."
    (Isa 46:11-12)

"And unless those days were shortened,
no flesh [people on Earth] would be saved;"
    (Matt 24:22)

"Watch therefore, and pray always
that you may be counted worthy to escape
all these things that will come to pass . . ."
    (Luke 21:36)

THE WARNINGS:

WE WILL KNOW
WHEN
WE ARE NEAR

"Go your way, Daniel,

for the words are closed up and sealed

till the time of the end . . .

and none of the wicked shall understand,

but the wise shall understand."

Dan 12:9-10

THE WARNINGS

"A prudent man foresees evil and hides himself;
the simple pass on and are punished."
Prov 27:12

*T*he Bible warns the darkest days of Earth's history are yet future ...

The events will be awesome and will strike suddenly. The events will be terrible. An unbelieving world will be taken by surprise. The devastation will be complete. The devastation will be global.

The Bible is clear in its warnings . . .

Please remember, while God promises *hope and an escape* to the believer, there will be *no* hope for those who reject Him. There will be no escape from the devastation. Fury will be unleashed upon the world. The fury will be relentless. The fury will be decisive.

Prophecies are placed in the Bible for a reason. Let's not be held accountable for ignoring them. Warning signs are given to help draw us near to Him for protection *before* the coming time of trouble . . .

We are told to *"Watch!"*

Why so many prophecies? Why so many warnings?

Because the Great Tribulation, the events which will someday sweep across the Earth, will be so terrible that God does not want *anybody* to have to go through it. That is why He stepped forth from Eternity for a moment in time two thousand years ago and "became flesh and dwelt among us," as the son of Man . . . as the Son of God. That is why He endured the pain, the shame, the torture, and the death on the Cross. He placed the guilt and the punishment of all of Man's sin *upon Himself.* He would take the full force of His Justice upon Himself, thus saving *any and all* who would simply *accept* it and believe it, in faith. That is why His offer is not to condemn or to judge the sinner, but to *save* . . .

However, all who *reject* God's offer will be held accountable.

While the terrors of the Apocalypse will come upon the world quickly and unexpectedly, those who wait in faith should *not* be taken by surprise -

> "But you, brethren, are not in darkness,
> so that *this Day* should overtake you as a thief.
> You are all sons of light and sons of the day.
> We are not of the night nor of darkness.
> *Therefore let us not sleep, as others do,*
> *but let us watch and be sober . . .*
> *For God did not appoint us to wrath,*
> but to obtain salvation through our Lord Jesus Christ"
>
> (1Thes 5:4-6,9)

THE SIGNS AND PROPHECIES

God said He would re-gather Israel back in the Land...

On May 14, 1948 God's prophetic clock started ticking again, *loudly*. These prophecies are important because we can now watch the news, read a book on post World War II history, or look at a current map of the world and see there is now a nation called Israel. For almost 2,500 years - starting with the Jewish captivity under Babylon, then Persia, then Greece, then Rome; and, almost 2,000 years since the birth and rejection of the Messiah, when God held the children of Israel accountable, and then, using the Roman army, scattered the people into the nations around the world - the Jews have been dispersed. A people without a nation. However, God said He would one day re-gather the children of Israel into the Land which He has given them as a nation. Through His prophets God also warned He would then judge them for profaning His holy name while scattered around the world. This prophetic re-gathering, which *this generation* is now seeing take place, is to serve *as a sign and a warning* to the world that the Apocalypse, the "Day of the Lord," draws near . . .

"He will set up a banner for the nations,
and will assemble the outcasts of Israel,
and gather together the dispersed of Judah
from the four corners of the Earth."   (Isa 11:12)

"Who has heard such a thing? Who has seen such things?
Shall the Earth be made to give birth in one day?
Or shall a nation be born at once?
For as soon as Zion was in labor, she gave birth to her children."
[Note: This prophecy *was* fulfilled *in one day* - on May 14, 1948]
    (Isa 66:8)

"*Thus says the Lord GOD:*
'Surely I will take the children of Israel from among the nations,
wherever they have gone,
and will gather them from every side
and bring them into their own land;'"
  (Ezek 37:21)

"And you, son of man, *prophesy* to the mountains of Israel,
and say, 'O mountains of Israel,
hear the word of the LORD ...'"
"But you, O mountains of Israel,
you shall shoot forth your branches
[note this for later prophecies]
and yield your fruit to My people Israel,
for they are about to come . . ."
"*For I will take you [Israel] from among the nations,*
gather you out of all countries,
and bring you into your own land."
  (Ezek 36:1, 8, 24)

Now, search through history for a nation Israel . . .

    Year   100?   "Nope."
    Year   300?   "Nope."
    Year   500?   "Nope."
    Year   900?   "Nope."
    Year 1200?   "Nope."
    Year 1500?   "Nope."
    Year 1700?   "Nope."
    Year 1800?   "Nope."
    Year 1900?   "Nope."
    Year 1948?   "*Yes!!!*" "*There it is . . . May 14, 1948!*"

How has the world reacted to such a profound fulfillment of Bible prophecy? A miracle that can be documented by simply looking at a map and a Bible. *It has ignored it!* Just as God says most of the world will ignore the warnings of the coming Apocalypse. Remember, God uses prophecy to *prove* that He is who He says He is, and to authenticate the warnings and the promises found in the Bible.

God said He would then make Jerusalem a trouble spot. A prophetic warning sign to the world . . .

"Behold, I will make *Jerusalem* a cup of trembling
unto all the people round about . . ."
(Zech 12:2 KJV)

"And *in that day* will I make Jerusalem
a burdensome stone for *all* people . . ."
(Zech 12:3 KJV)

Watch the news *anywhere in the world* to *see* these two prophecies being fulfilled. Then ask yourself . . .

"How many cities in the world are larger than Jerusalem?"

"How frequently do these *other* cities make world news?"

"Do these other cities *tremble* with so much anger as Jerusalem?"

Through these prophetic verses, God is telling us that *He* is the one who is making Jerusalem such a trouble spot today.

GAZA!!! A terrible warning ...

Gaza is in the land which was given to the tribe of Judah (Joshua 15:1-12), and one of Messiah's titles is "The Lion of the Tribe of Judah" (Revelation 5:5).

The Bible *links* GAZA to the coming "Apocalypse." Several years ago the world watched as *all* the Jews in Gaza were forcibly removed from their homes and their land ... even those buried in cemeteries were forcibly dug up from their graves and removed from Gaza. This 'uprooting' of the Jews from Gaza may be a much more 'significant' prophetic event than most realize ..

GOD has issued a terrible warning and a 'plea' to the children of Israel and to ALL people on Earth ...

"Gather yourselves together,
  Yes, gather together
  O undesirable nation
  Before the decree is issued,
  Before the day passes like chaff,
  Before the Lord's fierce anger
  comes upon you,
  Before the Day of the Lord's anger
  comes upon you!
  Seek the Lord,
  all you meek of the Earth
  who have upheld His justice
  (this warning includes *all* Mankind)
  Seek righteousness,
  Seek humility.
  It may be that you will be hidden
  In the Day of the Lord's Anger (Wrath)."
  (The coming 'Apocalypse')
  (Zephaniah 2:1-7)

2. GOD wants all in Israel and on Earth to know what will help trigger His fierce and terrible anger (the coming "Apocalypse"): GAZA!! He warns, 'Gaza will be forsaken' ... her inhabitants (the children of Judah) 'uprooted' and 'driven out.'

"For GAZA shall be forsaken,
  And Ashkelon desolate;
  They shall drive out Ashdod at noonday,
  And Ekron shall be uprooted.
  Woe to the inhabitants of the seacoast,
  The nation of the Cherethites!
  The Word of the Lord
  is against you, O Canaan,
  land of the Philistines (Palestinians):
  "I (God) will *destroy* you
  So there shall be no inhabitant."
('Palestinians' and allies should take note)
  (Zephaniah 2:1-7)

3. God ALSO wants all to know there is Hope. For one-day in the future, after the coming 'Apocalypse' (also called the 'Day of God's Fierce Anger') a remnant of the tribe of Judah will once again peacefully inhabit and prosper in that precious land God promised and gave to them ... For at that time, God will restore all the Earth in peace and beauty ... as promised.

"The seacoast shall be pastures,
  with shelters for shepherds and folds for flocks.
  The coast shall be for the remnant of the house of Judah;
  They shall feed there flocks there
  (in the coastlands of Gaza);
  In the houses of Ashkelon they shall lie down at evening.
  The Lord their God will intervene for them,
  And return their captives."
  (Zephaniah 2:1-7)

God sends an ominous warning to the generation which witnesses the re-gathering of Israel in the Land . . .

Jesus says, *"Now learn this parable from the fig tree [Israel]:"*
"When its branch has already become tender
and puts forth leaves, [Israel re-gathering in the land]
you know that summer is near.
Also, when you see all these things,
know that it is near-- at the doors!
Assuredly, I say to you, *this generation*
will by no means pass away
till all these things take place."
(Mark 13:28-30 - also see Matt 24:32-34, Luke 21:29-33)

Let's take a closer look at these important verses in order to get a better sense of the significance of what the Lord is trying to tell us, or more importantly what He is trying to *warn* us about . . .

1. Jesus says - *"Now learn this parable from the fig tree:"*

There are several places in the Bible where God uses the fig tree as an idiom for Israel.

2. *"When its branch has already become tender
and puts forth leaves, you know that summer is near."*

"And puts forth leaves . . . " This refers to Israel being re-gathered in the Land. This is a parable, so Jesus is painting a "word picture." The verses in Ezekiel 36 help us out by explaining to us that "shooting forth its branches" refers to Israel being re-gathered in the Land. Like a tree in winter, Israel has been lying dormant for about 2,000 years, looking dead and barren to the world. Then, in May of 1948 it sprang back to life and like the re-birth of a tree in springtime started "shooting forth its branches" . . .

We can now watch "its branch become tender and put forth leaves" as Israel has begun to prosper. Miraculously, this tiny nation of Israel is today one of the largest exporters of fruit and flowers in the world. Jesus is warning us that when we see these things, we should know that "summer is near," meaning we are close to His return, and that awesome and terrifying "final harvest," which prophet after prophet has cried out and warned against will soon be upon us.

3. *"Also, when you see all these things,*
    know that it is near-- at the doors!"

Can't you sense the urgency in His voice? We cannot comprehend the global destruction which will someday soon sweep across this world. Jesus gives these warnings because we are told that those who are alive and wait for Him in faith will be pulled out or "raptured" just before God's wrath is poured out on a violent and unbelieving world.

4. *"Assuredly, I say to you, this generation will by no means pass away"*

Q. Which generation?
A. The generation that sees Israel re-gathering back in the Land.

Q. Well, isn't that generation alive today?
A. I think so.

Q. How long is a generation?
A. I really don't know, but God answers most questions. Let's look at a couple of verses from Psalm 90, which is provocative in that it is the only Psalm written by Moses and seems to come out of nowhere . . .

"The days of our lives are seventy years;
And if by reason of strength they are eighty years . . .
who knows the power of Your anger?"
(Psalm 90:10,11)

Is then the *fullness* of a generation 70 - 80 years? Did a prophetic countdown start with the Nation in 1948, or when Israel regained control over their capital city of Jerusalem in 1967? We don't know. We are simply warned to "*Watch!*" We will never know the exact day or the hour. However, "this generation" which mocks God and His laws will someday soon know "the power of His anger . . ."

5. *"Till all these things take place."*

"All these things" means *everything* the Bible warns will happen before the promise of Christ's return, including the Rapture, the terrors of the Apocalypse . . . and Armageddon.

With such an ominous warning to the generation which sees Israel re-gathering in the Land, how else can we be certain we are in "that generation?"

As we will see in these next prophecies, God goes out of His way to tell us a *lot* about the generation who will be alive at the time of the Apocalypse. God wants us to know and to recognize the generation. God wants us to refuse to blindly follow that generation who will pull the world down into their darkness and into the awesome and terrifying "day of the Lord," also called the Apocalypse and the Great Tribulation . . .

96

The Apostle Paul provides a prophetic profile or "checklist" of the identifying character traits of "the generation" who will lead the world into the unspeakable terrors of the Apocalypse . . .

"But know this, that *in the last days*
perilous [savage, fierce] times will come,
for men will be -
    lovers of themselves,
    lovers of money
    boasters, proud, blasphemers
    disobedient to parents
    unthankful
    unholy, unloving, unforgiving
    slanderers, without self-control
    brutal [violent]
    despisers of good
    traitors, headstrong
    haughty [arrogant]
    lovers of pleasure rather than lovers of God
    having a form of godliness [professing a belief in "God"]
    but denying its power.
    And from such people turn away [shun, avoid]!"
      (2 Tim 3:1-5)

In Proverbs, God tells us even more about the character of this generation . . .

"There is a generation that curses its father,
and does not bless its mother.
There is a generation that is pure in its own eyes,
yet is not washed from its filthiness."
    (Proverbs 30:11-12)

God also provides prophetic insights into the mood and the attitudes of those who will be found living "in the last days" . . .

> "Knowing this first:
> that scoffers will come *in the last days*,
> walking according to their own lusts,
> and saying, 'Where is the promise of His coming?
> For since the fathers fell asleep, all things continue on
> as they were from the beginning of creation.'" (2 Pet 3:3-4)

What two things help characterize the attitude of "the last days?"

1. *"Knowing this first: that scoffers will come in the last days,*
   walking according to their own lusts,
   and saying, 'Where is the promise of His coming?'"

"The generation" will ridicule those who take the warnings of the Bible seriously and wait in faith. What will people "scoff" at? What events constitute "the promise of His coming?"

The world will scoff at those who believe . . .

– God will once again intervene and demonstrate His power over a world which denies Him, mocks His law, and rejects His grace.

– Jesus will return suddenly "as a thief in the night" to safely remove those who believe in Him, to shelter them from the carnage and devastation that will sweep across the globe sometime thereafter.

– Jesus will return a second time at the *end* of the Tribulation, restoring the Earth in innocence and purity, and to establish His Kingdom on Earth . . . a Kingdom of peace and beauty.

2. *"Knowing this first: that scoffers will come in the last days ...
saying ... 'For since the fathers fell asleep, all things continue
on as they were from the beginning of creation.'"*

The generation of the Apocalypse will blindly believe life will
simply "evolve" and continue on as always. The prophet Isaiah
offers even more insight into this attitude which will help identify
the generation of the Apocalypse . . .

Isa 56:12
    "Come," one says, "I will bring wine,
    and we will fill ourselves with intoxicating drink;
    tomorrow will be as today, and much more abundant."
[The philosophy of *our* generation and the path of destruction.]

However, through the Apostle Peter, God does graciously answer
those who *sincerely* ask, *"Where is the promise of His coming?"* or,
"It's been 2000 years, why hasn't He returned yet?"

    "The Lord is not slack concerning His promise,
    as some count slackness, but is longsuffering [patient] toward us,
    not willing that any should perish
    but that all should come to repentance."
    (2 Peter 3:9)

God is patient. We are told He has waited this long because He loves
us and wants us to repent, which simply means to change and turn
back to Him and His ways, which are good. He is filled with patience,
forgiveness, and mercy. He will protect and shelter all who will draw
close to Him before the coming time of trouble. He warns us through
prophecy so we will realize how perilously close we are to the end.
He wants us to realize how far from Him and His protection we have
wandered, and to run back to Him as we sense the danger we are in.

God compares "this generation" to the one of Noah . . .

Jesus warns, "But as the days of Noah were,
so also will the coming of the Son of Man be . . ."
(Matt 24:37)

**To help us understand this prophecy God describes
the generation of Noah . . .**

*"The Earth also was corrupt before God,
and the Earth was filled with violence.*
So God looked upon the Earth, and indeed it was corrupt;
for all flesh had corrupted their way on the Earth.
And God said to Noah, 'The end of all flesh has come before Me,
for the Earth is filled with violence through them;
and behold, I will destroy them with the Earth.'"
(Gen 6:11-13)

**And, "As in the days of Noah," worldly men and women will
casually ignore God's warnings and live as though God will never
intervene and life will simply continue on as always . . .**

Jesus said, "But as the days of Noah were,
so also will the coming of the Son of Man be."
"For as in the days before the flood,
they were eating and drinking,
marrying and giving in marriage,
until the day that Noah entered the ark,
and did not know until the flood came and took them all away,
so also will the coming of the Son of Man be." (Matt 24:39)
[The coming Apocalypse will strike suddenly and decisively.]

God warns "the generation" will be characterized by lying . . .

> *"But know this,*
> that *in the last days* perilous times will come . . . (2 Tim 3:1)
> Evil men and impostors [seducers]
> will grow worse and worse,
> deceiving [lying] and being deceived." (2 Tim 3:13)

The Scriptures tell us God cannot lie and He hates all liars. God says truth is non-negotiable and is fundamental to His law. In the past, liars and perjurers were dealt with harshly and severely. Today we see lying casually accepted and even presented as funny or harmless. In God's eyes, elected leaders of a democracy are mirrors which reflect the people who elected them and willingly keep them in office. As noted, telling the truth is fundamental to God's law. In the Bible we find when a nation and its leader(s) defiantly mock, ignore, and turn their backs on God's law, God will turn His back on that nation and remove His protection and blessings from that people. God help us. The future of that people and nation is usually very, very grim. The other distressing thing found in this prophecy is God warning us the deception and lying will continue to grow even worse and worse. The leaders of "this generation" will not only disobey and ignore God's laws but will even brand God's laws as "intolerant" and will somehow twist obedience to God's laws into "hate." Just watch.

Prophetic global "warning" trends . . .

The following verses are taken from a remarkable portion of Scripture found in the Gospels where Jesus sits down with four of His disciples and provides them (and us) with a sweeping outline of the future, in prophecy, as reported in Matthew 24, Mark 13 and Luke 21. This prophetic briefing is called the "Olivet Discourse" because it takes place on the Mount of Olives. Jesus hurtles us through time from the destruction of the Temple in 70 A.D. to His final return as the Christ, Lord of lords and King of kings, to establish His just rule on Earth.

101

Four disciples ask about the future . . .

"Now as He [Jesus] sat on the Mount of Olives,
the disciples came to Him privately, saying,
'Tell us, when will these things be?'
And 'What will be the sign of Your coming,
and of the end of the Age?'"
(Matt 24:3)

Here we find the sweeping *scope* of the prophecies Jesus is about to reveal. As we study this verse, we find there will be three specific divisions of the future addressed:

1. *"Tell us, when will these things be?"*

   This question refers to the prophecy Jesus had just given concerning the destruction of the Temple (Matt 24:2). We find the prophecies which answer this question reported and outlined in Luke's report of this prophetic discourse (Luke 19:41-44).

2. *"And what will be the sign of Your coming"*

   This question refers to the signs which will be given and the events which would take place before He returns for His church, "as a thief in the night," sometimes called the "Rapture," in order to shelter and protect those who believe in Him and still wait for Him in faith from those awesome and terrible events which will strike the world during that coming period of time Jesus calls the "Great Tribulation." It is *this* portion of prophecy we are reviewing in this section.

3. *"And of the end of the age?"*

This question refers to the signs and events which would take place before Jesus returns the *second* time, not as a "thief in the night," but when every eye "will see the Son of Man coming on the clouds of heaven with power and great glory." These will be the signs and events that will take place during that period of time Jesus calls the "Great Tribulation." This upcoming period of time called the "Great Tribulation" is given many names in the Bible and refers to the awesome events which will take place during a 3½ year period of time which represents the last half of a very specific 7 year period of time also known as the prophetic 70th Week of Daniel (a week of years = 7 years. See Daniel 9:24-). In the Book of Revelation (also known as the Book of the Apocalypse), John lists and details the awesome and terrible events which will strike suddenly and sweep over the Earth. The 7 years will start with a man who will rise to power first over Europe and then over the whole world. This coming world leader (the Antichrist) will enforce some treaty with Israel for a period of 7 years. Halfway through his enforcement of this treaty, or exactly 3½ years later (using prophetic 360 day years), this "man" (who will perform miracles and will be looked at by the world as the Messiah) will stand in the holiest place or room in a new Jewish Temple which will be built in Jerusalem and command that the world worship him as God. This event is technically and prophetically called the "abomination of desolation," and at that moment God will begin to pour out His wrath on an arrogant, unbelieving, and violent world, night and day, for exactly 3½ years, or exactly 1,260 days, during which most of the world will be utterly destroyed, *"And unless those days were shortened, no flesh would be saved."* After all these things take place, Jesus, the true Messiah (Christ), will then return.

Jesus answers His disciples and reveals the future . . .

> And Jesus answered and said to them:
> "Take heed that no one deceives you.
> For many will come in My name, saying, 'I am the Christ,'
> and will deceive many. And you will hear of wars
> and rumors of wars. See that you are not troubled;
> for all these things must come to pass,
> *but the end is not yet.*
> For nation [*ethnos*] will rise against nation [*ethnos*],
> and kingdom against kingdom.
> And there will be famines, pestilences,
> and earthquakes in various places.
> All these are the beginning of sorrows [*birth pangs*]."
>   (Matt 24:4-8)

This portion of Jesus' prophetic discourse reveals the signs and events which will lead up to His sudden return for His church, "as a thief in the night," sometimes called the "Rapture," to remove and shelter those who believe in Him and still wait for Him in faith from those awesome and terrible events which will sometime thereafter strike and engulf the world.

Jesus warns of global "birth pangs" before the Apocalypse . . .

1. *And Jesus answered and said to them:*
   "Take heed that no one deceives you.
   For many will come in My name,
   saying, 'I am the Christ,' and will deceive many."

Jesus warns we will see cults and false messiahs . . . *increasing.*

2. *"And you will hear of wars and rumors of wars.*
    See that you are not troubled;
    for all these things must come to pass,
    but the end is not yet"

    There will be no lasting peace until Jesus, the Messiah, returns.

3. *"For nation will rise against nation,"*

    The actual word used in the Greek which was translated "nation" was *"ethnos,"* from which we get our word *"ethnic."* Jesus is warning us we will see ethnic tension and violence . . . *increasing.*

4. *"And kingdom against kingdom."*

    We will see small and large wars around the globe . . . *increasing.*

5. *"And there will be famines,"*

    We will see hunger, starvation, and famines . . . *increasing.*

6. *"Pestilences [deadly diseases],"*

    We will see the spread of deadly diseases . . . *increasing.*

7. *"And earthquakes in various places."*

    We will see the number of global earthquakes . . . *increasing.*

8. *"All these are the beginning of sorrows."*

    The word translated "sorrows" actually means *"birth pangs."*

So, although the world has always had false messiahs, cults, wars, ethnic violence and strife, starvation, disease, epidemics, and earthquakes, Jesus tells us that *as a sign that we are entering into the last days* we will see each of these increase in frequency and size. Described as "birth pangs," these "pains" will continue to grow worse and worse, coming closer and closer together, as signs we are preparing to enter the Apocalypse . . .

And Jesus warns,
"For *then* there will be great tribulation, such as has not been since the beginning of the world until this time,
no, nor ever shall be [the Apocalypse].
And unless those days were shortened,
no flesh would be saved;"   (Matt 24:21-22)

Jesus tells us that *never* in the history of Mankind has there been anything as terrible on Earth as the coming Apocalypse, the "Great Tribulation" - only a small remnant of the world will survive.

Pride comes before a sudden fall (this includes powerful nations) -
Beware of "treaties," "land for peace," or promises of "security."
Devastation will come swiftly and silently as the world "sleeps" . . .

The Scriptures say there will be no lasting peace until Messiah returns.

"For you yourselves know perfectly
that the day of the Lord so comes as a thief in the night.
For when they say, "Peace and safety!"
then sudden destruction comes upon them,
as labor pains upon a pregnant woman.
And they [Israel and the nations of the world] shall not escape.
But you, brethren [believing Christians], *are not in darkness,*
so that this Day should overtake you as a thief."   (1 Thes 5:2-11)
[He expects us to be alert, aware, and recognize the warning signs]

Jesus warns we will see "lukewarm" Christians and churches whose love and faith in Christ will be "cooled off" by the contentment and sense of self-sufficiency that money and a good economy can bring. A stark and powerful warning is given . . .

Jesus says, "I know your works, that you are neither cold nor hot.
I could wish you were cold or hot.
So then, because you are lukewarm,
and neither cold nor hot,
I will vomit you out of My mouth. "
Because you say, 'I am rich, have become wealthy,
and have need of nothing'-- [money *will test the hearts* of people]
and do not know that you are wretched,
miserable, poor, blind, and naked . . .
And he who has an ear let him hear." (Rev 3:15-17, 22)
[And a good economy will test the heart of a nation]

The Bible warns as we approach the Apocalypse we would see an "apostasy" (falling away) or "corruption" from within the Church, when many churches would no longer teach sound doctrine . . .

"Beloved, while I was very diligent to write to you
concerning our common salvation,
I found it necessary [compelled] to write to you
exhorting you to contend earnestly for the faith
which was once for all delivered to the saints.
For certain men have crept in unnoticed, [church leaders]
who long ago were marked out for this condemnation,
ungodly men, who turn the grace of our God into lewdness . . .
[who will ignore, change, or deny God's law to appease the world]
But I want to remind you, though you once knew this,
that the Lord, having saved the people out of the land of Egypt,
afterward destroyed those who did not believe." (Jude 1:3-6)
[Never confuse God's patience with approval]

107

The Apostle Paul goes on to write . . .

> *"Now the Spirit expressly says*
> *that in latter times some* [religious leaders]
> *will depart from the faith,*
> giving heed to deceiving spirits and doctrines of demons,
> speaking lies in hypocrisy,
> having their own conscience seared with a hot iron,
> *forbidding to marry,*
> *and commanding to abstain from foods*
> which God created to be received with thanksgiving
> by those who believe and know the truth. *"*
>   (1 Tim 4:1-3)

The Bible warns angels would appear before men to change, pervert, or corrupt the true message of Christ . . .

> "I marvel that you are turning away so soon from Him
> who called you in the grace of Christ,
> to a different gospel, which is not another;
> but there are some who trouble you
> and want to pervert the gospel of Christ.
> But even if we, *or an angel from heaven,*
> preach any other gospel to you
> than what we have preached to you, *let him be accursed.*
> As we have said before, so now I say again,
> if anyone preaches any other gospel to you
> than what you have received, let him be accursed."
>   (Gal 1:6-9)

We are warned "false Prophets" would rise and deceptively lead
many people away from the truth . . .

> *"Then many false prophets will rise up and deceive many.*
> And because lawlessness [sin] will abound,
> the love of many [for Christ] will grow cold."
> (Matt 24:11-12)

A promise is given for all those who will endure in faith . . .

> *"But he who endures to the end shall be saved.*
> And this gospel of the kingdom will be preached in all the world
> as a witness to all the nations, and *then, the end will come."*
> (Matt 24:13-14)

So, beware of any who teach another Gospel, or anything that would
be in direct opposition to Jesus' Commandment to "Love others as
yourself," meaning, beware of those religions that would not treat
others just as they would want to be treated, even their enemies . . .

There are religions today who teach they must convert the world "by
the sword," even using terror. It is important to note that God, the true
God of Abraham and Isaac, never *forces* Himself on anyone. Never
in the Bible does Jesus Christ try to force anybody to believe in Him
or to attend His church. Jesus simply says that He "Stands at the door
and knocks." We have to open that door. God tells us that He has
given each and every man and woman a free will to decide for
themselves whether or not to accept His Offer of salvation through His
Son, Jesus Christ. He clearly outlines the choice, and sincerely warns
us of the consequences. It is a personal decision. God says that He
looks at each man and woman's heart to see if they are sincere in their
belief. Christ is looking for people to come to Him out of love. If a
man or woman ever decides not to believe in Jesus, that is their
choice. It saddens God for He knows what their destiny will be after
they die. But, never does He ask others to force a non-believer to
return, or try to force them into believing through threats of injury or

death. God shows us the only places we will find these coercive conversion tactics are from those who are driven by a depraved spirit and the dark power of Satan. God says the Bible is His Word. The Bible says God cannot lie and God says He will never change. The Bible has withstood the test of time. God challenges every religious system to hold the words of their books, their leaders, their founders, their prophets and their angels up to the light of truth. God welcomes all to search His Scriptures and try to find error, contradictions, or lies. He also includes many, many prophecies to authenticate His Word. If you belong to a religion, or church, that follows a prophet or worships a god who is so small and insecure that he would have people threatened with death if they criticize or refuse to join, and will threaten people with death or bodily harm if they decide to leave through their own free will, *then flee!* If you follow a religion or belong to a church that is afraid to hold the people who founded the religion or the words they spoke and the books they ask you to believe, up to the light of truth, *then flee!* God's warning to the non-believer is clear. But God also tells us clearly that we are not to judge others, for they will be judged by Him after our earthly bodies die. God looks directly into the heart of each man and woman to see what each truly believes. Only a strange, twisted, paranoid religion, driven by the dark and evil powers of Satan himself would ever rape, torture, kill, imprison, beat, kidnap, behead, bomb, burn alive, or harm people in any way as a means to convert or to force people into joining, or staying, in their religion. The god of *that* religion *is not, and never has been,* the God of Abraham. *Any* religion that would do these things is *not* lead by the Holy Spirit of God. It is a religion of darkness. It is a religion of evil, twisted, wicked men, directed and lead by the power of Satan.

Many blessings are promised in Heaven to those who withstand such religions and suffer or die in their faith for doing so. Remember, *Christianity is a relationship with God and Jesus* . . . not a religion.

God has warned He is re-gathering His people, the children of Israel, back in their land as a sign and for judgement. He tells us why . . .

We are told through the prophet Ezekiel that God has not re-gathered the Jews in their Land because they deserve it, but because God's name and His Word are at stake. This means He is doing it because He *said* He would do it. The Bible tells us Israel is being re-gathered for punishment and for judgment. God, however, says the rest of the world will not go unpunished (see the prophecies of Armageddon). God explains that while the Jews have been scattered and dispersed among the nations, they have profaned His Holy name and have rebelled against His laws . . .

Ezekiel 36:17-23

> "Son of man, when the house of Israel dwelt in their own land,
> they defiled it by their own ways and deeds;
> to Me their way was like the uncleanness of a woman
> in her customary impurity.
> Therefore I poured out My fury on them
> for the blood they had shed on the land,
> and for their idols with which they had defiled it.
> *So I scattered them among the nations,*
> *and they were dispersed throughout the countries;*
> I judged them according to their ways and their deeds.
> [this prophecy *was fulfilled* around 70 A.D.]
> When they came to the nations, wherever they went,
> they profaned My holy name--
> when they said of them, 'These are the people of the LORD,
> and yet they have gone out of His land.'
> *But I [God] had concern for My holy name,*
> which the house of Israel had profaned among the nations
> wherever they went."

111

"Therefore say to the house of Israel,
Thus says the Lord GOD:
'I do *not* do this [re-gather Israel in the Land] *for your sake,*
O house of Israel, *but for My holy name's sake,*
which you have profaned among the nations wherever you went.
And I will sanctify [set aside] My great name,
which has been profaned among the nations,
which you have profaned in their midst . . .'"
[Strong warnings. God's key word in these verses is *"profane."*]

Let's look in the Bible at two activities that God <u>Himself</u> links to profaning His Holy Name . . .

Leviticus 18:21-22
"And you shall not let any of your descendants [children]
pass through the fire to Molech,
Nor shall you profane the name of your God: I am the LORD.
You shall not lie with a male as with a woman.
It is an abomination."

What are these activities God links to profaning His Holy Name?

1. **Abortion.** *Passing descendants (babies) "through the fire."*
   Also known and described as the worship of Molech . . .

Do a study of Molech and "passing children through the fire" in the Bible and you will find they refer to sacrificing babies for pleasure and convenience. Today we call this baby sacrifice "abortion." In ancient days people would place a small statue in a fire until the arms of the statue turned red hot and started to glow. Then, an unwanted baby would "pass through the fire" by having the priest (doctor) place the small baby on the glowing arms in the fire in order to kill, or "offer" this unwanted baby to Molech, the "god" of pleasure (convenience is a form of pleasure).

112

Although our methods and technology have changed, the result and the intent are the same - abortion is sacrificing a baby to a god of pleasure and convenience. If you study this abomination and profane activity of abortion - "passing children through the fire" (worshiping Molech) in the Bible, you will find it not only incites and angers God, but it also deeply affects and grieves Him . . .

"Were your acts of harlotry a small matter,
that you have slain *My* children
[notice God looks upon these little, slain, babies as *His*!]
and offered them up to them [to *other* gods]
by causing them to pass through the fire?"   (Ezek 16:20-21)
[choosing to worship another god *is* the choice in "pro-choice"]

2. **Homosexuality.** *Men lying with men as a woman.*

The Bible is not ambiguous in its message concerning homosexuality. God never judges anybody or calls for capital punishment against anything that is simply "genetic." God never calls anything "profane" or an "abomination" if it is a genetic defect. Homosexuality is not new. When we study the passages concerning Sodom and Gomorrah, it appears homosexuality, or sodomy, is symptomatic of a people who have willfully rejected and defiantly mock God's laws in order to do "that which is right in their own eyes." Sodom and Gomorrah are given as warnings.

Please remember, our God is a forgiving God who will forgive any and all who have sinned against Him. *Any* sinner, including those who have walked the path of homosexuality or have had an abortion, can be lovingly forgiven and washed clean through the blood of the Lamb. Jesus died for *all* sinners. And we are *all* sinners. God hates the sin, but He loves and cares for the sinner. He pleads with all of His lost sheep to stop and repent from doing those things that are wrong, and *with tears of joy* He will richly forgive and welcome all back with the open arms of a loving Father.

The reason it is important to take such a long look at these verses is because *this generation* is unique in making homosexuality and abortion *their* issue. In the Bible, God says these activities are wrong. This generation says God is wrong. So, in order to approve of or accept these things, one must deny God. The prophets warned we would see a generation rise who would do just this. While most of us would simply like to ignore these things, we can't. Incredibly, *special* rights are being proposed which would lift these groups *above* the average citizen. When we look at those who advocate and promote these activities, we even find many who call themselves Jewish and Christian at the forefront, angrily accusing anyone who believes these activities are wrong of being filled with "hate" or "intolerance." The homosexual movement has risen to become one of the most powerful forces in this nation. Look at the spreading AIDS epidemic. AIDS is the first *politically protected* contagious and fatal disease in the history of this nation. Who is protecting the civil rights and the safety of the *uninfected?* Although our heart goes out to those who are sick, and they must be cared for, we must also protect the uninfected. Laws which were passed in earlier generations to protect against deadly and infectious diseases are being ignored. This generation is lifting up powerful judges over this land, even at the highest level, who willfully promote and advocate homosexuality and abortion - activities which *the God of the Bible, the God of Israel Himself,* calls "abominable," and "profane," as they hand down judgements which are in *direct opposition* to God's law. In this generation we find church leaders allowing practicing homosexuals to be ordained as shepherds over their flocks, and powerful Jewish leaders loudly promoting abortion. As we just read in Ezekiel, God is aware and conscious of these things. Not since the deepest depravity of Ancient Rome has a single generation so mocked and ignored God's laws and warnings in such a willful and disobedient way. Our God is a forgiving God, but we sadly find He will turn His back on a nation and a people who have turned their backs on Him. The prophets warned we would see this willful disregard for God's laws, which the Bible calls "lawlessness," as we quickly approach the Apocalypse.

114

***The Bible warns the generation which approves of these things will
be held as accountable as those who do these things . . .***

"For the wrath of God is revealed from heaven against
all ungodliness and unrighteousness of men . . .
For even their women exchanged the natural use
for what is against nature [lesbianism].
Likewise also the men, leaving the natural use of the woman,
burning in their lust for one another,
men with men committing what is shameful [homosexuality] . . .
that those who practice these things
are worthy of death [*thanatos* - bodily, or spiritual death in Hell]
not only those who do the same but
also **approve of those** *who practice them!"* (Rom 1:18, 26, 27, 32)
[Note: Many *other* offenses are listed in addition to those listed here.]

As with any sin, there are people caught up in these activities who are
struggling in their effort to stop and to change. We, as Christians, are
to love them and help them in any way we can. We are *all* sinners.

***God warns those who mock God's law by saying those things which
God calls evil are good, and those which are good are evil . . .***

"Woe to those who call evil good, and good evil;
who put darkness for light, and light for darkness;"
[Many will learn the "woes" of God are very real.]
(Isa 5:20)

***The heart of Jesus is filled with love for little children. His love is
so great He offers an ominous warning to any who would cause
them to sin, including educators who would teach our children the
"do's and don'ts" of the Bible are wrong or no longer valid in
today's world . . .***

115

"Then Jesus called a little child to Him,
set him in the midst of them, and said,
'Assuredly, I say to you, unless you are
converted and become as little children,
you will by no means enter the kingdom of heaven.
Therefore whoever humbles himself as this little child
is the greatest in the kingdom of heaven. Whoever receives
one little child like this in My name receives Me. *But*
whoever causes one of these little ones who believe in Me to sin,
it would be better for him if a millstone were hung around
his neck, and he were drowned in the depth of the sea.
Woe to the world because of offenses! For offenses must come,
but woe to that man (or woman) by whom the offense comes!"
    (Matt 18:2-7)

God warns us not to be seduced by the attitudes of the world.
Do not casually embrace the fads, the celebrities, the philosophies,
the politics, or any of the other "gods" of this world.
It "ain't cool" in God's eyes . . .

"Do not love the world or the things in the world.
If anyone loves the world,
the love of the Father is not in him.
For all that is in the world--
the lust of the flesh, the lust of the eyes, and the pride of life --
is not of the Father, but is of the world."
    (I John 2:15-16)

"Do you not know that friendship with the world
is enmity with God?
Whoever therefore wants to be a friend of the world
makes himself an enemy of God."
    (James 4:4)

The world is powerful. It despises the Cross. "The world" can be seen and heard 7 days a week, 24 hours a day on *CNN*, MTV, ABC, CBS, NBC, PBS, HBO, Time Warner, Buena Vista (Disney) Pictures, etc, etc, etc, speaking through the shows we watch, the music we hear, and the things we read. The world speaks powerfully from the Media centers of Hollywood, New York, Atlanta, San Francisco, and others. A deadly spiritual virus flows from these centers and infects all that it touches. It blinds and numbs our soul. The only inoculation against this deadly virus is through the blood on the Cross. We can open the door of our hearts and invite Jesus Christ into our lives, allowing the innocence, the goodness, the honesty, and the purity of His word and spirit to flow through our veins. He is our only protection.

We are in a spiritual battle . . . we are the battleground.

Sadly, most of us are no longer taught in many of our churches or synagogues to discern, or even *care* to discern good from evil. It's tough. Movies, television, music, magazines, and newspapers are all a major part of our lives. These are the new pulpits and podiums of the world. Each can powerfully change, shape, and form our attitudes and beliefs, yet we are seldomly allowed to see or get to know the people who actually create the characters and write the words . . .

Watch television, read a newspaper, read a book, watch a movie. When you finish, think back to which character, group, or person you were told, taught, or directed to like, approve of, or feel sorry for, and then think back to the character, group, or person you were left hating, disliking, or disapproving of. Ask your children which character they thought was good and which character they thought was evil, or which character they would like to be like. Now, consider and look at how the writer, actor, or director, subtly shaded, lighted, and presented each character. A month from now will you remember, or will your children remember, that the evil character was a "reverend of the cult of celestial ..." or will your children only remember that the wicked, evil character looked like a church minister wearing a red or white collar on his neck. Watch where the director places a Cross in a scene, or how each person who prays or quotes Scripture is depicted. Watch for "miracles" such as a "virgin birth" or Biblical "plagues" in a movie. Who are we left believing performed these miracles? As with Eve in the Garden, many things which are seductively offered to entertain us and are "pleasant to the eyes" will attack our faith in God, the Bible, and Jesus by subtly planting seeds of doubt or confusion. Our thoughts, our beliefs, our likes, and our dislikes are dictated by that which we see, hear, watch, and read, and how each idea, character, or belief is presented. This is why an advertiser will pay *millions* of dollars for only a few seconds of "air time" during a Super Bowl. In just a few seconds they know they can effectively begin to subconsciously direct our likes and dislikes. One powerful tactic in "mind manipulation" is to use a person who appears wise, attractive, funny, or popular as the spokesperson. Another powerful tactic is to add "children" to a photo, a message, or a cause. Associating children with a person or cause is a widely used method of *manipulating* public opinion. Another successful tactic is to find a spokesperson who is angry, loud, or shrill - a person who will mock, ridicule, and interrupt anyone whose ideas they fear and whose ideas they cannot compete with, in truth. These tactics are very effective in manipulating the minds of the audience. Also, the younger the audience is, the more vulnerable they are to such powerful psychological manipulation. *The most transparent and subtle attacks on your opinions and beliefs are the most powerful and effective.* This is why so many things which the Bible says are wrong and against God's law are now casually accepted and even promoted as good. You or your children can easily be de-sensitized to even the worst evil if it is presented in the right way. Look again at the characters in your last movie, television show, book, or news broadcast, and see who was lifted up as good or smart and who was cast as evil, or ridiculed. Consider how subtly, artfully, and effectively the characters were cast, portrayed, and presented to you. Now, consider sincere Christians, who simply believe in Jesus Christ and are taught to do their best to respect and obey God's laws.

How is the Christian portrayed in your movie, television show, book, or news broadcast? The Bible warns that Satan, who is also called "the prince of the power of the air," will plant seeds of hate and doubt into your mind whenever and wherever he has a chance. *It works!!!* Just say the words "Jesus Christ" or "born again Christian" and see how you feel inside. Has the world successfully made you feel ashamed, unwelcome, afraid, or embarrassed to be called a Christian?

Jesus says, *"If the world hates you,*
you know that it hated Me before it hated you.
If you were of the world, the world would love its own.
Yet because you are not of the world,
but I chose you out of the world, therefore the world hates you."
    (John 15:18-19)

Jesus prayed, "I have given them Your word;
and the world has hated them
because they are not of the world,
just as I am not of the world.
I do not pray that You should take them out of the world,
but that You should keep them from the evil one [Satan]."
[As noted earlier, Satan is also called the *"ruler* of this world"]
    (John 17:14-15)

We can now see the separation between believing Christians and "the world," including the rapidly changing definition and division of "church and state," gaining momentum every day. Events will take place that will be unjustly blamed on Christians and laws will be passed with deceptive names and titles which will come down hard, *very* hard on anybody who will stand firm in their faith and stand firm in their obedience to the Bible and God's law. The mocking and ridicule of believing Christians will continue to heighten to higher levels of vehemence and frenzy until someday soon when it will take a much darker, and violent turn . . .

119

The door of escape will soon close . . .

The Lord has clearly warned us. He warned there would be a generation who will pull the world down into their darkness. He says if we turn from our arrogance and stop worshiping and casually accepting the violence, lies, gross immorality, greed, and selfishness; and if we simply return to Him and His ways, which are good, with a sincere and humbled heart, He will relent and withhold that which is about to strike the Earth . . .

"If my people, *which are called by my name,*
shall humble themselves,
and pray, and seek my face,
and turn from their wicked ways;
then will I hear from heaven,
and will forgive their sin, and will heal their land."
    (2 Chr 7:14)

"Before the decree is issued, before day passes like chaff,
before the LORD'S fierce anger comes upon you,
before the day of the LORD'S anger comes upon you!
Seek the LORD,
all you meek of the Earth, who have upheld His justice.
Seek righteousness, *seek* humility.
It may be that you will be hidden
in the day of the LORD'S anger."
    (Zeph 2:2-3)

There is a day and an hour which no man knows but the Father . . .

*"I [the Lord] have held My peace a long time,
I have been still and restrained Myself.* [God's patience *will* end]
*Now I will cry like a woman in labor . . .
I will lay waste the mountains and hills"*
    (Isaiah 42:14-15)

*"I will punish the world for its evil,
and the wicked for their iniquity;
I will halt the arrogance of the proud"*
    (Isaiah 13:11)

Jesus offers His final warnings . . .

He [Jesus] answered and said to them [religious leaders],
"When it is evening you say,
'It will be fair weather, for the sky is red;'
and in the morning,
'It will be foul weather today, for the sky is red and threatening.'
Hypocrites! You know how to discern the face of the sky,
but you cannot discern the signs of the times." (Matt 16:2-4)
[Jesus was rebuking them *for blindly ignoring the prophecies.*]

"When you see all these things,
know that it is near -- at the very doors!"
[The terrors of the Apocalypse draw near.]
    (Matt 24:33)

"And what I say to you, I say to all: *Watch!"*
    (Mark 13:37)

121

God's Warning To Me . . .

"When I say to the wicked, 'You shall surely die,'
and you give him no warning, nor speak to warn the wicked
from his wicked way, to save his life,
that same wicked man shall die in his iniquity [sin];
but his blood I will require at your hand.
"Yet, if you warn the wicked, and he does not turn
from his wickedness, nor from his wicked way,
he shall die in his iniquity;
but you have delivered your soul.
"Again, when a righteous man
turns from his righteousness and commits iniquity,
and I lay a stumbling block before him, he shall die;
because you did not give him warning, he shall die in his sin,
and his righteousness which he has done shall not be remembered;
but his blood I will require at your hand.
"Nevertheless if you warn the righteous man
that the righteous should not sin, and he does not sin,
he shall surely live because he took warning;
also you will have delivered your soul."
  (Ezek 3:18-21)

ANOTHER <u>AMAZING</u> MATHEMATICAL PROPHECY

The Promised Return of Israel . . .

The prophecies found in the Bible are very interesting and remarkable, both in the way in which they are presented and in their incredible accuracy. To help simplify this translation, we will use the Living Bible translation from Tyndale House . . .

> Ezekiel 4:4-6
> "Then God said to Ezekiel,
> 'Now lie on your left side for 390 days,
> to show that Israel will be punished for 390 years
> by captivity and doom. Each day you lie there
> represents a year of punishment ahead for Israel.
> Afterwards, turn over and lie on your right side for forty days,
> to signify the years of Judah's punishment.
> Each day will represent one year.
> You are to bear their sin for the number of days
> you lie on your side.'" (The Living Bible, paraphrased)

Although perhaps a little obscure (and sophisticated), this is one of the most fascinating mathematical prophecies found in the Bible.

Here we find God telling Ezekiel that each day he (Ezekiel) lies on his side will represent a year of punishment for the nation of Israel (Judah) because of their iniquities (sins) against God . . .

So, we have 390 days + 40 days = 430 days.
We are told the 430 days represent 430 *years* of judgement.

In 606 B.C. Israel (Judah) was taken into captivity by Babylon for exactly 70 years . . .

$$430 \text{ years}$$
$$\underline{- 70 \text{ years}}$$
$$360 \text{ years}$$

There should have been a total of 360 years left in judgement against Israel after their return. Bible scholars could not find any specific captivity or dispersion that fulfilled these 360 years, *until* a close look in the book of Leviticus revealed a startling prophetic warning . . .

"And after all this, if you do not obey Me,
then I will punish you *seven times more* for your sins."
     (Lev 26:18)

"Then, if you walk contrary to Me, and are not willing to obey Me,
I will bring on you *seven times more* plagues,
according to your sins."   (Lev 26:21)

"And after all this, if you do not obey Me,
but walk contrary to Me,
then I also will walk contrary to you in fury; and I,
even I, will chastise you *seven times* for your sins."
     (Lev 26:27-28)

"I will scatter you among the nations
and draw out a sword after you;
your land shall be desolate and your cities waste."
     (Lev 26:33)

The 7X factor of God's judgement. God warned Israel if they continued in their disobedience *He would multiply their judgement by seven times!* Remember, as noted earlier, God says what He means and means what He says. Now, let's *apply* this 7X factor to the remaining 360 years of judgement against Israel in this remarkable mathematical prophecy:

360 x 7 = 2,520 years of judgement remaining

To convert the 360 day Babylonian/Persian years into our 365.25 day solar years, first multiply:

2,520 $_{years}$ x 360 $_{days}$ = 907,200 days of judgement

To convert these days into years, divide by 365.25 (.25 for leap years):

907,200 $_{days}$ ÷ 365.25 = 2,483.78 years

With this information, let's again look at this remarkable prophecy:

606 B.C.	Israel taken into Babylonian captivity
- 70 $_{years}$	for 70 years.
= **536 B.C.**	End of the first 70 years of judgement
+ 2483 $_{years}$	Now add the 2,483 years left in judgement
+ 1 $_{year}$	Add 1 year because of no "0" A.D. or B.C.
= **1948 A.D.!**	End of judgement against nation Israel

Judah (Israel) was taken into captivity by the Babylonians in 606 B.C. They were released from captivity 70 years later by the Persians, in 536 A.D., *exactly* as Jeremiah had prophesied, but their land was still under the control of the Persians. The Persians were later conquered by the Greeks, and the land of Israel remained under Greek control. The Greeks were then conquered by Rome and the land of Israel remained under Roman control. After a failed rebellion against Rome around 70 A.D., the Romans removed the Jews from the land and dispersed them around the world. Then, for the first time since the Babylonian captivity in 606 B.C., the world watched as Israel once again appeared on the map as a sovereign nation, on *May 14, 1948 - exactly when the Bible said it would!*

Have doubts?
Make a checklist ... then watch!

- ☐ Israel in the Land again as a Nation ... *wake up call!!!*
- ☐ Jerusalem, a *"cup of trembling," a "burdensome stone."*
- ☐ Iran and allies threatening war against Israel.
- ☐ Russia rising ... and acting as a "guard" for Iran
- ☐ China with weapons capable of destroying 1/3 of Mankind
- ☐ Ethnic tension and brutal ethnic wars . . . *increasing.*
- ☐ False Prophet(s) . . . *increasing.*
- ☐ Diseases and epidemics . . . *increasing.*
- ☐ Strong earthquakes in various places . . . *increasing.*
- ☐ Europe . . . strong mixed with weak nations uniting as one.
- ☐ Some kind of extraordinary sights or signs from space.
- ☐ A generation identified by the following characteristics:
  - Lovers of themselves
  - Lovers of money . . . boasters . . . proud
  - Blaspheming and mocking the names of God and Jesus
  - Disobedient to parents
  - Unthankful . . . unholy . . . unloving . . . unforgiving
  - Without self-control
  - Brutal . . . taking pleasure in violence
  - Despising things that are good . . . traitors
  - Headstrong . . . refusing to submit to authority
  - Arrogant . . . lovers of pleasure
  - Having a *form* of godliness [professing a belief in "God"]
- ☐ A generation characterized by lies, selfishness . . . *violence.*
- ☐ A generation turning away from God . . . mocking His Laws.
- ☐ Hatred rising . . . Christians being blamed for random acts.
- ☐ Apostasy. "Lukewarm" churches corrupting from within.
- ☐ Jerusalem! A call to battle. *All* nations will turn against Israel.

"When you see all these things, know that it is near-- at the doors!"
(Mark 13:29)

MESSIAH

HIS RETURN

"Then I saw heaven opened,
and behold a white horse.
And He who sat on him was called
Faithful and True,
and in righteousness
He judges and makes war"

"And He has on His robe and on His thigh
a name written:
KING OF KINGS AND LORD OF LORDS."

Rev 19:11,16

CHRIST, THE KING RETURNS

*T*he Bible tells us that Jesus Christ, the Messiah, will return *twice* -

- *First,* "as a thief in the night" - *for* those who waited in faith.
- *Second,* "every eye shall see" - *with* those who waited in faith.

We believe a *minimum* of 7 years will separate these two events . . .
The prophecies of the Apocalypse must be fulfilled before His return.
We are told much will happen during this period of time which will
separate the Rapture from Christ's return, including:

- The U.S. "neutralized". . . Israel must stand alone - with God.
- A Russian invasion of Israel with Iran and Moslem allies.
- A 10 nation European alliance will rise in power.
- A leader will exert control over these nations - *the Antichrist.*
- *Empire.* This Leader will gain control over the whole world.
- A world "Spiritual" leader will also rise . . . out of *Rome.*
- One Religion emerges . . . global worship . . . Satanic power.
- Slaughter of Christians who come to Christ *after* the Rapture (the millions who will die are promised blessings in Heaven).
- "The Beast". . . the world Leader will declare himself "God" while standing in a newly built Jewish Temple in Jerusalem.
- From that moment the Tribulation will last *exactly* 1,260 days.
- A Great War will ignite the world.
- Terror and death will fall from the heavens.
- Fire and destruction will engulf the Earth.
- The weapons *will* be used . . . cities and nations will disappear.
- All living creatures in the oceans and seas will die.
- Only a small remnant of the world will survive.
- The final battle . . . Armageddon.

There will be no question it is Him . . .

Jesus warns there will be false Prophets and messiahs who will rise from the population on Earth. However, Jesus says when *He returns* to rule there will be *no question* it is Him. When He again steps forth from Eternity *every* eye will see Him "coming in the clouds" with millions from Heaven, in power and great glory . . .

"Then if anyone says to you,
'Look, here is the Christ!' or 'There!'
do not believe it.
For false christs and false prophets will arise
and show great signs and wonders [miracles]
so as to deceive, if possible, even the elect.
See, I have told you *beforehand.*" [Meaning - *this is a prophecy*]
"Therefore if they say to you,
'Look, He is in the desert!'
do not go out;
or 'Look, He is in the inner rooms!'
do not believe it.
For as the lightning comes from the east and flashes to the west,
so also will the coming of the Son of Man be."
   (Matt 24:23-27)

"Behold, He is coming with clouds,
and every eye will see Him,
even they who pierced Him.
And all the tribes of the Earth will mourn because of Him . . ."
   (Rev 1:7)

Christ Returns:
This is His promise . . . this is our hope.

He has told us to wait for Him in faith. He has told us to warn others.
Now, let us listen to the Holy Spirit as He prepares the way . . .

"And I will pour on the house of David
and on the inhabitants of Jerusalem
the Spirit of grace and supplication;
then they will look on Me whom they have pierced;
they will mourn for Him as one mourns for his only son,
and grieve for Him as one grieves for a firstborn."
    (Zech 12:10)

"Therefore wait for Me," says the LORD,
Until the day I rise up to plunder [attack the prey];
my determination is to gather the nations
to My assembly of kingdoms,
to pour on them My indignation,
all my fierce anger [during the Great Tribulation];
all the Earth shall be devoured with the fire of My jealousy.
For *then* I will restore to the peoples a pure language,
[for the first time since the Tower of Babel in ancient Babylon]
that they all may call on the name of the LORD,
to serve Him with one accord."
    (Zeph 3:8-9)

"Then the sign of the Son of Man will appear in heaven,
and then all the tribes of the Earth will mourn,
and they will see the Son of Man coming on the clouds of heaven
with power and great glory." (Matt 24:30)

"Now Enoch, the seventh from Adam,
[the first person *"raptured"* in the Bible]
also prophesied about these men, saying, *'Behold,*
the Lord comes with ten thousands [millions] of His saints,
to execute judgment on all, to convict all
who are ungodly among them of all their ungodly deeds
which they have committed in an ungodly way,
and of all the harsh things which ungodly sinners
have spoken against Him.'" (Jude 1:14-15)

"For behold, the LORD will come with fire and with His chariots,
like a whirlwind [a global hurricane of fire],
to render His anger with fury, and His rebuke with flames of fire.
For by fire and by His sword the LORD will judge *all* flesh;
and the slain of the LORD shall be many." (Isa 66:15-16)

"I was watching in the night visions, and
behold, One like the Son of Man, [Jesus]
coming with the clouds of heaven!
He came to the Ancient of Days,
and they brought Him near before Him.
Then to Him was given dominion and glory and a kingdom,
that all peoples, nations, and languages should serve Him.
His dominion is an everlasting dominion,
which shall not pass away, and
His kingdom the one which shall not be destroyed."
    (Dan 7:13-14)

"The Earth is violently broken,
[the Earth will *reel* under the power of His return]
the Earth is split open,
the Earth is shaken exceedingly.
The Earth shall reel to and fro like a drunkard,
and shall totter like a hut;
its transgression shall be heavy upon it,
and it will fall, and not rise again." (Isa 24:19-20)

"And *in that day* [the Day of the Lord]
His feet will stand on the Mount of Olives,
which faces Jerusalem on the east.
And the Mount of Olives shall be split in two,
from east to west . . .
It shall come to pass in that day
that there will be no light; the lights will diminish.
It shall be one day which is known to the LORD--
neither day nor night.
But at evening [night] time it shall happen that it will be light."
[Awesome]   (Zech 14:4, 6, 7)

"Now it shall come to pass *in the latter days . . .*
He shall judge between the nations,
and rebuke many people;
they shall beat their swords into plowshares,
and their spears into pruning hooks;
nation shall not lift up sword against nation,
neither shall they learn war anymore." (Isa 2:2,4)

"*At that time Jerusalem* [the same Jerusalem you see on the news]
shall be called the Throne of the LORD,
and all the nations shall be gathered to it,
to the name of the LORD, to Jerusalem.
No more shall they follow the dictates of their evil hearts."
    (Jer 3:17)

"*He will be great,*
and will be called the Son of the Highest;
and the Lord God will give Him the throne of His father David.
And He will reign over the house of Jacob forever,
and of His kingdom there will be no end."
    (Luke 1:32-33)

"From Jesus Christ, the faithful witness,
the firstborn from the dead, [speaking of His Resurrection]
and the ruler over the kings of the Earth.
To Him who loved us
and washed us from our sins in His own blood,
and has made us kings and priests to His God and Father,
to Him be glory and dominion forever and ever. Amen.
Behold, He is coming with clouds,
and every eye will see Him,
even they who pierced Him.
[not as a "thief in the night" this time]
And all the tribes of the Earth will mourn because of Him.
Even so, Amen."
    (Rev 1:5-7)

He will return with millions and millions of those who believed and waited in faith . . .

"And they sang a new song, saying:
'You [Jesus] are worthy to take the scroll,
and to open its seals;
for You were slain,
and have redeemed us to God by Your blood
out of every tribe and tongue and people and nation,
And have made us kings and priests to our God;
and we shall reign on the Earth.'
Then I looked,
and I heard the voice of many angels around the throne,
the living creatures, and the elders;
and the number of them was
ten thousand times ten thousand,
and thousands of thousands,
[these represent *millions upon millions* of faithful believers]
saying with a loud voice:
'Worthy is the Lamb who was slain
to receive power and riches and wisdom,
and strength and honor and glory and blessing!'"
    (Rev 5:9-12)

Awesome . . .

"Now I saw heaven opened, and behold, a white horse.
And He who sat on him was called Faithful and True,
and in righteousness He judges and makes war.
His eyes were like a flame of fire,
and on His head were many crowns.
He had a name written that no one knew except Himself.
He was clothed with a robe dipped in blood,
and His name is called The Word of God.
And the armies in heaven, clothed in fine linen,
white and clean, followed Him on white horses.
Now out of His mouth goes a sharp sword,
that with it He should strike the nations.
And He Himself will rule them with a rod of iron.
He Himself treads the winepress of the fierceness
and wrath of Almighty God.
And He has on His robe and on His thigh a name written:

KING OF KINGS AND LORD OF LORDS."

(Rev 19:11-16)

The Holy Spirit has spoken to us in prophecy
as a true and faithful witness.

AFTER THESE THINGS

THE SEPARATION: HEAVEN OR HELL

THE KINGDOM AGE . . .

AND BEYOND

*"For God did not send His Son
into the world to condemn the world,
but that the world through Him
might be saved.*

*He who believes in Him
is not condemned;
But he who does not believe
is condemned already,
because he has not believed in the name
of the only begotten Son of God."*

John 3:17-18

HEAVEN OR HELL: THE SEPARATION

Every person has a soul,
and every soul will be judged . . .

Why were we created? What is the purpose of life?
The Bible tells us we were created *for the Lord's good pleasure.*

> "Thou art worthy, O Lord, to receive glory and honor and power:
> for thou hast created all things, and *for thy pleasure*
> they are and were created." (Rev 4:11 KJV)

The "real" life God has prepared for us will not start until *after* this
body dies. It appears from the Scriptures this short life is merely a
test, and God is using this time to separate the "wheat from the chaff"
and the "sheep from the goats," separating those people who *want* to
be with Him in His Kingdom of Heaven . . .

> "At the time of harvest I [Jesus] will say to the reapers,
> 'First, gather together the tares and bind them in bundles to burn
> them, but gather the wheat into my barn.'" (Matt 13:30)

> "When the Son of Man comes in His glory,
> and all the holy angels with Him,
> then He will sit on the throne of His glory.
> "All the nations will be gathered before Him,
> and He will separate them one from another,
> as a shepherd divides his sheep from the goats.
> "And He will set the sheep on His right hand,
> but the goats on the left.
> "Then the King [Jesus] will say to those on His right hand,
> 'Come, you blessed of My Father, inherit the Kingdom prepared
> for you from the foundation of the world:'" (Matt 25:31-34)

139

The Bible tells us there will actually be three judgements: One for the Believer, one for the Non-believer, and one for the that small remnant of people who will still remain scattered around the nations when Jesus returns. We will focus on the first two judgements . . .

- *The judgement for the believer:*
  All who believe in Jesus and accept His death on the Cross as payment, or pardon, for all their sins.

- *The judgement for the non-believer:*
  The great White Throne judgement for all who reject Jesus Christ, thus refusing His pardon.

The problem is most people don't believe or won't believe they will really be judged *after* they die. It is a fearful thing so most people simply deny it, trivialize it, or just ignore it . . .

> *"And as it is appointed for men to die once,*
> but *after this* the judgment*"*
> (Heb 9:27)

Remember, God has gone to incredible lengths to make it simple for us to enter into His Kingdom. His offer is free and it is not based on our righteousness or "goodness," but on His. He took our punishment for us. He died to provide our way into His Kingdom of Heaven. He died to save us from Hell. *He paid the debt for all of our sins.* Jesus took our sin and guilt *upon Himself.* Our debt, *paid in full,* by Him. All we have to do is accept it by sincerely believing in Him, in faith.

The Bible says Jesus *is* the door . . . the *only* door into Heaven. The Cross is our doorway into Heaven and it is His blood on the Cross that washes us clean from all those things we have ever done, said, thought, or felt, that are wrong. His blood on the Cross will protect us from the *second* death which we are told is the agony and torment of Hell. The Bible is either true or it is false . . . there is no in between.

"For God so loved the world that He gave His only begotten Son,
that whoever believes in Him should not perish [in Hell]
but have everlasting life [in Heaven].
For God did not send His Son into the world to condemn
the world, but that the world through Him might be saved.
He who believes in Him is not condemned;
but he who does not believe is condemned [to Hell] already"
  (John 3:16-18)

"If you confess with your mouth the Lord Jesus
and believe in your heart that God has raised Him from the dead,
you will be saved [His Kingdom of Heaven]." (Rom 10:9)

"The Son of Man will send out His angels,
and they will gather out of His kingdom all things that offend,
and those who practice lawlessness [sin],
and will cast them into the furnace of fire.
There will be wailing and gnashing of teeth." (Matt 13:41-42)

"For what profit is it to a man if he gains the whole world,
and is himself [his soul] destroyed or lost?
For whoever is ashamed of Me and My words,
of him the Son of Man will be ashamed . . ." (Luke 9:25-26)

"Also I say to you, whoever confesses Me before men,
him the Son of Man also will confess before the angels of God.
But he who denies Me before men
will be denied before the angels of God." (Luke 12:8-9)

"So it will be at the end of the age.
The angels will come forth,
separate the wicked from among the just,
and cast them into the furnace of fire.
There will be wailing and gnashing of teeth." (Matt 13:49-50)

Judgment for those who believe in Christ:
The punishment for our sins . . . *paid in full* on the Cross

- All who have *accepted* God's offer of Grace and forgiveness through His Son, Jesus Christ.

- Any and *all* who sincerely *believe in* and *accept* Jesus as Lord.

- This judgment is for those who will inherit the Kingdom.

- Each will still be held accountable for every word and action.

- Each will be judged on *how we obeyed His commandments.*

- Each will be judged on *how we served Him and honored Him.*

- Each will be judged on *how we treated other people.*

- Each will be judged on *how we loved and forgave others.*

- Each will be judged on *patience and gentleness.*

- Each will be judged on *how we served and shared with others.*

- There will be rewards for good works . . .
  For humbly helping and selflessly sharing with others.

- We then enter into our rest . . .

- An eternal life of peace and beauty.

- A *new* life . . . an *eternal* life in God's Kingdom of Heaven.

Judgment for the Non-believer:
All who did not believe in Jesus or *accept* Him as their Savior

- Every man and woman who rejects God's offer of Grace *by rejecting* His Son, Jesus Christ.

- This is called the great "White Throne" Judgment.

- *"But whoever denies Me before men, him I will also deny before my Father."*

- *"For whoever is ashamed of Me and My words, of him the Son of Man will be ashamed."*

- Each who stands here will be judged . . . and condemned.

- *Finality* . . . the door is then closed . . . *forever.*

- The Bible warns being cast into Hell is the death we should fear.

- Condemned . . . eternal darkness . . . alone . . . "separation."

- Eternal . . . torment . . . wailing . . . gnashing of teeth.

- It is solely based on *your* decision to accept Him or reject Him.

- *He cares!* He died rejected, bleeding, nailed to a Cross - for *you!*

- There is no "soul sleep" . . . no second chance . . . no reincarnation.

THE CHOICE OF YOUR ETERNAL DESTINY IS MADE BY *YOU* . . .

NOT BY GOD

THE KINGDOM AGE

Although the Bible clearly warns the darkest days of Earth's history are yet future, the Bible *also* promises the most peaceful and restful days of Earth's history are also in the future. We are promised a most incredible Age on Earth unlike anything the world has ever experienced since the days in the Garden of Eden, when Adam and Eve still walked with God. Satan, also called the "ruler of this world" and the "god of this Age," now inflicts the world with violence, fear, heartbreak, sickness, and death. Christ defeated Satan at the Cross and will someday soon return to take possession of that which is His. We are told the Earth will be fully restored to an innocence and beauty we can't imagine and we will be allowed to live in it and enjoy it for a thousand years . . . the Millennium.

The Holy Spirit drops a few hints in the Bible concerning this future Kingdom Age as He provides a small peek into the future . . .

> *"He will swallow up death forever,*
> and the Lord GOD will wipe away tears from all faces;"
> (Isa 25:8)

> "The wolf also shall dwell with the lamb,
> the leopard shall lie down with the young goat,
> the calf and the young lion and the fatling together;
> and a little child shall lead them.
> The cow and the bear shall graze;
> their young ones shall lie down together;
> and the lion shall eat straw like the ox.
> The nursing child shall play by the cobra's hole,
> and the weaned child shall put his hand in the viper's den.
> They shall not hurt nor destroy in all My holy mountain,
> for the Earth shall be full of the knowledge of the LORD
> as the waters cover the sea . . ."
> (Isa 11:6-9)

"Then the eyes of the blind shall be opened,
and the ears of the deaf shall be unstopped.
Then the lame shall leap like a deer,
and the tongue of the dumb sing.
For waters shall burst forth in the wilderness,
and streams in the desert.
The parched ground shall become a pool,
and the thirsty land springs of water;"
    (Isa 35:5-7)

"The wolf and the lamb shall feed together,
the lion shall eat straw like the ox . . . "
    (Isa 65:25)

The pain, the fears, the loneliness, the emptiness, and the tears will be wiped away from all who endure in faith and wait patiently . . .

Then, the Bible takes us <u>beyond</u> the Kingdom Age . . .

"Now I saw a new heaven and a new Earth,
for the first heaven and the first Earth
had passed away . . ." (Rev 21:1)

According to the Bible, there will be a time when this Earth will be "replaced." It even describes the new world that is being prepared. Mysterious, impossible to comprehend, and exciting - all at the same time.

Do not worry or be anxious . . .

God's Amazing Grace. We are saved by faith in Him . . . no added rules.

- Jesus paid the debt for *all* of our sins ... our old sins and new sins.
- Just believe in Him with all of your heart.
- Savior. Jesus says He saves us from the *second* death, the torment of hell, which we are told follows a judgement *after* this life.
- We are saved from this by a simple faith in Jesus.
- Jesus willingly took the penalty and punishment for *all* your sins when He died alone and rejected . . . nailed to a wooden Cross.
- He completed *all* of the work on the Cross. You cannot add to it.
- Just as those who looked at the bronze serpent Moses put on the pole were saved (see Numbers 21:9), so shall those who look upon the Messiah hanging on the Cross be saved.
- Demonstrate faith by changing your life. Respect and honor Jesus.
- Obey Him by learning of God and loving God. He has earned it.
- Obey Him by treating others as you would want to be treated.
- Admit your sins to God in prayer. He lovingly forgives all things.
- *All* of your sins *will be forgiven* . . . through His son, Jesus Christ.
- Sincerely try to stop doing those things which are wrong.
- Do not dishonor Jesus by feeling embarrassed for your belief.
- Simple faith and belief ... no additional works, rituals, or donations of money can save you.
- Nor can you be saved by or through *any other person* regardless of their title or position.
- It is simply your relationship with Jesus . . . *trust in Him.*
- He will not turn *anybody* away. We will all fail Him many times.
- There *will be* heartbreak, trials, pain, sickness, death and much difficulty in *this* life.
- Concerning the coming time of trouble . . . *do not fear* . . . simply hold fast to your faith in Christ . . . He will lovingly protect you.

COMFORT FOR THE BELIEVER

GOD'S

PROMISE

GOD'S PROMISE . . .

It has been said that for those who believe in Jesus this life will be the closest thing to Hell that we will ever experience. But, for those who don't believe, this life will be the closest thing to Heaven . . .

Jesus died rejected and alone on the Cross. The Bible, God's Word, tells us that it was not the nails which were driven through His hands and feet that kept Jesus on the Cross, it was His love for you. He willingly and lovingly took the penalty and punishment for *all* of your sins. Each and every one of them, regardless how big or how small. Your debt, *paid in full, by Him.* Through God's grace, you simply need to *accept* it and *believe* it. It is free to everybody. It is available to everybody. But, God has given each of us the free will to make our own choice. We must *choose* to accept it. We must choose to believe it. It has to be a conscious decision made by each of us at some point in our life. If, through prayer, we simply and sincerely admit or confess that we have sinned, ask for God's forgiveness, and accept Jesus Christ as our Lord and Savior and His death on the Cross as payment for our sins, regardless of how bad our sins are or how often we have sinned or how long it has been since we have asked for God's forgiveness (a simple, short prayer) and sincerely believe these things, it is not only His Word and Promise that all of our sins will be forgiven and completely forgotten, but God tells us that it is the *only* way we can be forgiven and enter into His Kingdom. He will forgive our failures and has compassion. He will help us to change and be strong when we need to be strong and He will be there and help us through all of life's battles . . . if we ask Him.

The Bible tells us that every man and woman on Earth is *already* condemned to Hell - "the second death." We are told the execution of this judgment will take place *after this body dies.* God also tells us there is an escape for *any and all* who will simply accept it . . .

149

God has gone to extraordinary lengths and pain to make it simple for us to escape the judgement of Hell. Jesus completed *all* of the work for us. We cannot enter Heaven because of the good deeds we have done, or *think* that we have done. We cannot enter Heaven because we were baptized as a baby, or were confirmed into a church. There is no other person here on Earth, regardless of their title, affiliation or position who can save us, and there is no ritual or donation of money that can provide entrance into Heaven, or provide an escape from the alternative. The gospel (good news) is that *if we simply believe* in our hearts that Jesus is the Christ (Messiah), and that Christ died for *all* of our sins, and that He was buried, and rose again the third day, and ask Him to come into our life as Lord and Savior . . . then, our life after death *is certain.* For if we acknowledge the King, we shall enter His Kingdom. If we deny the King, we shall be denied entrance into the Kingdom. The Kingdom of Heaven . . . life, an eternal life, beyond anything we can *ever* imagine . . . ***it's God's Promise and His Word.***

It is simply our faith in Jesus Christ. Faith in His blood on the Cross, *accepting* His blood on the Cross as full payment for all of our sins. It covers our guilt and guarantees our life in His Kingdom of Heaven.

The "all roads and religions lead to heaven" or "I've been a good person, so I'll go to Heaven" philosophies are wrong and deadly. Three times Jesus prayed in the garden just before His Crucifixion, "If it is possible (if there is ***any other way***), then let this cup (His death on the Cross) pass from Me." *"No one comes to the Father except through Me"* (John 14:6). There is *no other way* into the Kingdom other than through Jesus Christ and His righteous blood on the Cross. If there *was* any other way, then He didn't have to die in agony on the Cross. He is the *only* door into Heaven. There is no window. You see it has *nothing* to do with how good we are (or think we are), or have been, *but only through our faith* in Jesus Christ. We are saved through *His* righteousness, not ours. This is God's grace, His gift to us. All *we* have to do is make a sincere decision to accept it.

150

The Bible tells us God loves each of us so much that He thinks about us constantly, day and night. His thoughts of us outnumber the grains of sand. A love so deep for us that He even allowed (and watched, heartbroken) His Son, His only begotten Son, sent forth from Heaven, willingly suffer and die *for us* (through an act of love, strength, and courage that is beyond our ability to comprehend), so that *any* who believe in Him will not die, but will enter into His Kingdom, through His righteousness, and will share in His glory and inheritance. *But,* He has given to each of us the free will to make our own decision to accept or reject His offer. He loves us and His wish is that *all* would accept His offer. That is why He has made it so simple for us and why it is based on His grace and not our "goodness," lest any of us should brag, or get a little "puffed up." All we have to do is *accept* it and *believe* it. If we sincerely ask Him into our lives, He will do the rest.

This short period of time which we have on Earth simply gives us the time to choose our own destiny. *Where* we will spend our eternity is *our* decision, not His. The moment our soul or spirit is released when this body dies, we will be both conscious and aware of the decision we made, or didn't make. *It is our own decision.* God tells us that belief comes through faith, not logic or intellect, and that our acceptance of His *gift* to us, through Christ, comes through faith (Heb 10-12). Jesus says that "you are either with Me or against Me" . . . *there is no in between.* He also says that if we call Him Lord, then we should obey Him, follow His commandments, and stop doing those things that are wrong. He will help us and He will forgive us whenever we fail . . . *if we ask Him.*

To have some doubts, or to not immediately understand everything is normal. As the Apostle Paul tells us, "We can see or understand only a *little* about God now, as if we were peering at His reflection in a poor mirror, or looking through a glass, darkly. All that we know now is hazy and blurred, but then (*after this body dies*) we will see everything clearly." (1 Cor 13:12, paraphrased)

If you sincerely ask Jesus into your life, He will reveal Himself to you, and will welcome you into His everlasting Kingdom. His Kingdom is so beyond our ability to comprehend that Paul tells us that there *are no human words* that can describe its peace and beauty.

Most of us have a conception that eternity "is just lots of time." This concept is wrong. Eternity, in God's Kingdom, is *disconnected* from our physical property of time (a concept that Einstein and quantum physics have helped us to understand, *a little*). It will be incredibly beautiful, peaceful, exciting, restful, never ending . . . *never boring!* It is interesting that science is finally catching up to the incredible accuracy and precision of the Bible, written over thousands of years, yet perfectly consistent. The Bible is God's proof of His existence and proof of His love for each of us, including His gracious offer of citizenship in His Kingdom, as sons and daughters, as co-heirs. All we have to do is accept His offer, through His Son, Lord Jesus Christ.

He will be there to welcome us . . . ***it's God's promise.***

The Lord's Comfort

The LORD is my shepherd, I shall not want.
He maketh me to lie down in green pastures,
He leadeth me beside the still waters.
He restoreth my soul.
He leadeth me in the paths of righteousness
for His name's sake.

Yea, though I walk through the valley
of the shadow of death,
I will fear no evil . . . for thou art with me.
Thy rod and thy staff they comfort me.

Thou preparest a table before me
in the presence of mine enemies.
Thou anointest my head with oil,
my cup runneth over.

Surely goodness and mercy shall follow me
all the days of my life . . .
and I will dwell in the house of the LORD
forever.

Psalm 23 (KJV)

"About the time of the end,

a body of men will be raised up

who will turn their attention to

the prophecies of the Bible

and insist on their literal interpretation

in the midst of much clamor

and opposition."

- Sir Isaac Newton -

(1643-1727 A.D.)

Resources

In preparing this work, I have drawn heavily from a number of different teachers and resources. Although the following list is sorely incomplete, each has tape and study resources which are highly recommended . . .

1. David Hocking, "Hope for Today"
   (800) 752-4253   www.hopefortoday.org

2. Chuck Smith, Sr. (Calvary Chapel), "The Word for Today"
   (800) 272-9673 www.thewordfortoday.org

3. Chuck Missler, Koinonia House
   (800) 546-8731 www.khouse.org

4. J. Vernon McGee, "Through the Bible"
   (800) 652-4253 www.ttb.org

In depth Bible studies are available on each book in the Bible, including many powerful prophecy studies and other topics. You can easily call for a list of available studies. Find out if there is a daily or weekly radio broadcast available in your area, or talk with the leader of your church to see what resources he might recommend.

For those of you who have made it this far, I pray that the Lord will reward you for your diligence, desire to learn, and hard work. Open the door of your heart now and invite Him in to enjoy the comfort and the blessings He will gladly and abundantly share with you.

God Bless

Made in the USA
Middletown, DE
11 April 2016